COOPER, Carina

The working cook

the working cook

Quick recipes for busy people

Carina Cooper

In association with the
Evening Standard

To: my grandmothers, my mother, my daughters

First published in 2006 by Collins,
an imprint of HarperCollins Publishers
77–85 Fulham Palace Road
Hammersmith
London W6 8JB

The Collins website address is www.collins.co.uk

Collins is a registered trademark of HarperCollins Publishers Ltd

12 11 10 09 08 07 06
7 6 5 4 3 2 1

Photographer: Peter Cassidy
Food Stylist: Sunil Vijayakar
Props Stylist: Roisin Nield
Design: Smith & Gilmour, London
Editor: Norma MacMillan

A catalogue record for this book is available from the British Library.

ISBN-13 978-0-00-721943-8
ISBN-10 0-00-721943-1

Printed and bound in China by Imago.

Author's acknowledgements

A huge thank you to all of the following, for the indispensable role that each and every one of you have played: Veronica Wadley and Anne McElvoy of the *Evening Standard*, my agent Lizzy Kremer, Denise Bates and her crew from HarperCollins – Zia Mattocks, Norma MacMillan, Peter Cassidy, Sunil Vijayakar, Roisin Nield and Smith & Gilmour. Thanks also to all my friends and acquaintances who have inspired me; and finally to my daughters, Ithaka, Flynn, Sidonie and ZaZou, the rest of my family and John Stockdale.

Contents

Introduction

We all know that the greatest commodity, these days, is time. Everybody seems to be rushed off their feet. People don't even sit down to eat, let alone shop and cook, too. It's all about attitude: try to enjoy choosing and buying food; see cooking as meditative and creative, and eating as satisfying and rewarding. I'm a busy mother with four children and I don't want to think of the kitchen as an area of burden – it should be a place of comfort, to elevate the spirits; it's my favourite room, the heartbeat of the house.

The intention of this book is to give you **straightforward**, **quick recipes** that will provide you with a **delicious**, **easy meal**, without needing to spend hours shopping and slaving in the kitchen. Whether you are cooking a nourishing supper for yourself after a long day at work, or feeding family or friends and wish to give the impression that you've put in a little more effort than you actually have, there's a recipe for every occasion and to suit all tastes, from fish to meat to veg, salads to soups to sweet treats.

I have divided the recipes into seven chapters: **1 Ultra-Fast** – meals that can be prepared and cooked in 20 minutes or less, for when you have very little time or inclination to cook (although you will find many other quick recipes throughout the book, as well as several where you can do some of the preparation in advance); **2 Feeling Virtuous** – light and healthy dishes for when you're watching your waistline; **3 Vegetarian** – recipes for those who don't eat meat, poultry or fish; **4 Indulge** – richer comfort food that is guaranteed to make you feel good; **5 Friends for Supper** – delicious easy dinners that look more elaborate than they are; **6 Sunday Lunch** – good, simple food for friends and family, such as casseroles and roasts; and **7 Sweet Things** – puddings, tarts, pies and cakes.

In general, the recipes in chapters 1 to 3 serve one to two people, while those in chapters 5 to 7 serve four to six; chapter 4 contains a mixture of each, but you can easily scale any of these quantities up or down as you desire. Quantities are often general – such as a handful of this or that – so that cooking can be a little instinctive and you can follow your own tastes and preferences. For some recipes I have suggested **alternative ingredients** that would work just as well as whatever is specified, such as John Dory instead of snapper, for example, in case you can't source the former. Where appropriate, I've also suggested **variations** and other **easy ideas** for both cooking and serving, to give you more options. Most of the recipes are **versatile** and **adaptable**, so have fun experimenting.

To speed things up further I have included some suggestions for ingredients to keep in your storecupboard (see pages 6–9). These are the things that I use most in cooking, so if you have most of these, you will only need to pick up a few fresh items on your way home in order to cook any of these recipes.

Whenever you're cooking, look to your ingredients first and foremost. The difference between a tomato grown hydroponically in Holland in December and one ripened on the vine in Italy in June is like that between a desert and a meadow. If you start off with **good, fresh, seasonal ingredients** – organic if possible – you have every chance of creating a delicious and memorable meal. I buy **organic** ingredients whenever I can. There is less wastage and I know I'm not eating pesticides, insecticides and other poisons – and it tastes better. I only ever buy organic **meat**, and I choose organic **eggs**, **fruits** and **vegetables** whenever possible. On Saturdays I like going to my local farmer's market, and buying fruit and vegetables from there; often they are organic, but if not they are from a smallholder and haven't been sprayed. I use a lot of skins of fruits and vegetables in my cooking, as that's where the **flavour** is, and I know this is the **healthier** option.

We all have our own culinary catalogue. Every time I prepare food, I leaf through my mental scrapbook of **tastes** and **influences** – the memories of dishes I've eaten, the **colours** or **sensations** of food I've tasted. I've travelled a great deal, so I have had an opportunity to try all kinds of cuisines. I'm a great user of **herbs** – they are the jewels that give a dish its sparkle – and I urge all cooks to cultivate their own herb garden, so they are always to hand. I cook from the heart and gut, and I hope that everyone who reads this book will develop the confidence to trust their **instincts** in the kitchen and to enjoy the process of working with food. After all, food sustains life and celebrates living.

> 'Look to your ingredients first and foremost. If you start off with good, fresh, seasonal ingredients – organic if possible – you have every chance of creating a delicious and memorable meal.'

Storecupboard

I use the term storecupboard loosely, meaning the essential provisions that you really should have in your kitchen. As well as using them as part of recipes, they are there so you can rustle up a meal when the fridge is empty – which means canned tomatoes, tomato purée, pasta, rice, cans of tuna in oil, Parmesan and the like. My list includes standard ingredients that I recommend you have in your storecupboard, to make your cooking both easier and more instinctive. I have divided it up into different categories so you can identify your absolute musts among other items that you might want only for certain styles of cooking, or that can be bought on a 'when needed' basis. If you cook regularly, you will soon begin to realise which ones you favour. The ingredients that I am never without are indicated by an asterisk.

Oils & fats

* **extra virgin olive oil** (Greek olive oil is ideal for everyday cooking; I use a more expensive Tuscan or French olive oil for salad dressings)
* **sunflower oil**
* **sesame oil**
groundnut oil
walnut oil
* **unsalted butter** (salted butter is too harsh)

Seasoning, sauces & flavourings

* **sea salt** (Maldon is my choice, as it doesn't burn the tongue; I cannot cook without it.)
* **black, green and pink peppercorns** (dry pack, never in brine. Pink peppercorns have a divine distinctive perfumed flavour that especially complements fish. I rarely cook with black pepper, as it leaves a strong fiery taste which fights with the subtlety of other flavours, so I mostly use it just before eating)
* **vegetable bouillon powder** (I recommend Marigold, which makes really good-quality vegetable stock with a flavour that doesn't interfere with other ingredients. It is also free from MSG stabilisers and flavour enhancers)
* **wine vinegars, both white and red** (I don't go in for fancy vinegars – they're too gimmicky)
* **balsamic vinegar** (the best is from Modena. To make balsamic vinegar taste as though it has been aged, boil a bottle with a glass of red wine and a tablespoon of soft brown sugar; simmer slowly until it becomes syrupy. This is delicious in salads, soups and sauces)
* **fish sauce**, either Thai (Nam Pla) or Vietnamese (Nuoc Mam), ideally Squid brand
* **soy sauce** – I only ever buy Kikkoman or Clearspring Organic Shoyu Soy Sauce
* **Worcestershire sauce** (I use this in Welsh rarebit, shepherd's pie and bloody Mary's)
Tabasco sauce
chilli sauce
* **tomato purée** (buy a good Italian make)
* **canned tomatoes** (again, an Italian brand is preferable)
* **organic tomato ketchup** (you can't have chips or burgers without ketchup. I favour Heinz)
* **horseradish**
* **capers**
anchovy fillets
* **mustard** (go for the three main ones – Dijon, grainy and English – it has to be Colman's)
* **garlic** (every summer I buy strings of garlic in France and hang them up in the kitchen)
onions – white, red and spring shallots
Cream or crème fraîche

Flour

* **plain flour** (choose organic)
* **easy-blend dried yeast**
* **self-raising flour** (buy organic)
cornflour

DE CECCO
Linguine ·7

Sweeteners & sweet flavourings

* **unrefined sugar**, both caster and granulated (it's not artificial or bleached, and not quite as sweet as normal white sugar)
* **soft brown muscovado sugar**

icing sugar

cocoa powder (I favour Green and Black's)

vanilla extract

* **honey** (runny and thick, ideally Seggiano)
* **redcurrant jelly** (this is my secret ingredient for gravy, stews, casseroles and soups)

Herbs

I can't cook without herbs; they are what pull a meal together for me. Grow them in pots or buy them fresh. I never use dried herbs – with the exception of tarragon and Greek or Sardinian oregano. My favourites are:

* **basil** – grow different varieties
* **thyme**

oregano

tarragon

* **coriander**
* **flat-leaf parsley**

sage

* **mint**
* **chives**

Spices

Spices have a long shelf life, so you can build up your collection as your cooking repertoire increases. These are some of my favourites:

* **cinnamon, both sticks and ground**
* **saffron threads**
* **vanilla pods**

star anise

* **cumin**, both seeds and ground

coriander seeds

fennel seeds

* **cardamom pods**

mustard seeds

ground allspice

celery seeds

China spice

chilli flakes

* **pimentón** (smoked sweet paprika)

paprika

* **mace**
* **cloves**
* **turmeric**

Pastas, grains & pulses

* **pasta** – spaghetti, penne, linguini and fusilli are a good basic supply (I buy good durum semolina wheat pasta; I don't like fresh pasta, except for ravioli and gnocchi)
* **rice** (short-grain Italian white, such as Arborio or Carnaroli, or short-grain Spanish Calasparra rice, for risotto or rice pudding; Thai or jasmine rice for Asian dishes; basmati rice for tagines and some curries; Camargue rice – organic red rice)
* **couscous**

polenta

lentils (Puy, red and yellow)

Alcohol

sherry

* **vodka** (keep it in the freezer)

vermouth

brandy

Marsala

Things to throw away

packs of gravy browning
cans, bottles or cartons of sauces
fake lemon juice
artificial sweeteners
canned or prepared garlic
canned vegetables (except tomatoes)
bottled salad dressing
artificial butter

one
ultra-fast – prepare and cook in 20 minutes or less

Lobster on chicory leaves with vodka dressing

SERVES 1-2 / PREP TIME: 10 MINUTES / COOKING TIME: 10 MINUTES

Lobster always feels like an extravagant indulgence, but sometimes it's good to treat yourself, even when it's not a special occasion. Cooked lobster tails are easy to buy from most fishmongers and are also often found in the freezer compartments of the supermarket. A vodka dressing snazzes everything up. I'd recommend getting out the shot glasses and swigging back some vodka to merry everything along.

2 Rosevalle or other waxy potatoes, cut into cubes
1 cooked lobster tail
1 spring onion, finely chopped
Maldon salt
1 red chicory
8 teaspoons extra virgin olive oil
grated zest of 1/2 lemon
2 teaspoons lemon juice
2 teaspoons vodka
1 teaspoon caster sugar

Cook the potatoes in boiling salted water for 7–8 minutes or until tender; drain and cool quickly under cold running water. While the potatoes are cooking, remove the lobster meat from the shell and chop finely.

In a bowl, mix together the lobster meat, potatoes and spring onion, and season with salt. Lay out six to eight chicory leaves on a plate and spoon the lobster mixture into them. Put the olive oil, lemon zest and juice, vodka and sugar in a jam jar or bowl. Combine well, then drizzle over the leaves.

Watercress, green bean & chicory salad with a prosciutto & prune dressing

SERVES 2 / PREP TIME: 15 MINUTES / COOKING TIME: 5 MINUTES

This is a rich, satisfying salad with a punchy dressing. Even so, it may not be sustaining enough for some, so I recommend serving some peeled, boiled potatoes tossed with an excess of chopped parsley on the side. A fabulous crisp white wine will go well.

a handful of thin green beans, such as Kenyan beans
4 tablespoons extra virgin olive oil
juice of 1/2 lemon
4 slices of prosciutto, finely chopped
2 prunes, finely chopped
2 spring onions, finely chopped
1 garlic clove, finely chopped
Maldon salt
freshly ground black pepper
1 head chicory, torn into pieces
a bunch of watercress, tough stalks discarded

Steam the green beans for 5 minutes or until al dente, then allow to cool.

Meanwhile, in a salad bowl, combine the olive oil, lemon juice, prosciutto, prunes, spring onions and garlic. Season well with salt and pepper. Add the chicory and toss to coat well in the dressing, then toss in the watercress.

When the beans have cooled to warm, toss them into the salad. Check the seasoning, then serve.

Sliced pork sausages with Thai leaf salad

SERVES 2 / PREP TIME: 10 MINUTES / COOKING TIME: 15 MINUTES

For pork sausages, go to a butcher and buy home-made ones, as these will impart a more meaty flavour to the salad. Alternatively, if you are passing a Chinese supermarket buy the sausages from there, as well as the fish sauce. Look for Thai basil and mint in Asian shops. I think this dish calls for a chilled Thai beer to drink with it.

4–6 pork sausages
2 servings of mesclun or other mixture of salad leaves
a small bunch of fresh Thai basil, chopped
a small bunch of fresh Thai mint, chopped
3 spring onions, cut lengthways into shreds (use the green stalks)

Dressing
1 teaspoon light brown sugar
2 teaspoons fish sauce
2 tablespoons toasted sesame oil
grated zest and juice of 1 lime
Maldon salt
freshly ground black pepper

Preheat the grill to moderate or the oven to 190°C/gas 5. Grill or roast the sausages until they are evenly browned and crisp.

Meanwhile, combine the mesclun or other salad leaves, basil, mint and spring onions in a serving bowl. To make the dressing, put the sugar, fish sauce, sesame oil, and lime zest and juice in a jam jar and give it a good shake. Season to taste with salt and pepper.

Slice the sausages, arrange them over the leaves and add the dressing. Toss well and serve immediately.

Salami, mozzarella, mint & broad bean salad

SERVES 2 / PREP TIME: 15 MINUTES / COOKING TIME: 5 MINUTES

This is a delicious little summer salad. The only fiddly bit is skinning the broad beans. If you make a nick in the skin of each bean at the black line, this not only helps the beans cook more quickly, but also makes it easier to squeeze them out of their skins once they are cooked.

a large handful of shelled broad beans
14 black Provençal olives, pitted and roughly chopped
10 fresh mint leaves, shredded
2 spring onions, roughly chopped
200g fresh buffalo mozzarella, cut into cubes
100g Italian sweet salami, sliced and each slice quartered
a few fresh chives

Dressing
2 tablespoons extra virgin olive oil
2 teaspoons red wine vinegar
a pinch of caster sugar
Maldon salt
freshly ground black pepper

Steam the broad beans for about 5 minutes, then drain and refresh them under cold running water. Remove the skins and set aside.

Combine the olives, mint leaves, spring onions, mozzarella and salami in a salad bowl. For the dressing, put the olive oil, red wine vinegar, sugar and salt and pepper to taste in a jam jar. Shake well, then pour over the salad and toss well. Divide the salad among two serving plates, place the broad beans on top and snip over the chives.

Goat's cheese quesadillas

SERVES 2 / PREP TIME: 10 MINUTES / COOKING TIME: 4-5 MINUTES

Normally when I cook quesadillas I make a filling with Cheddar cheese, tomatoes, avocados, and so on – the classic Mexican filling. This is a little bit of a twist on that. Use a soft spreadable goat's cheese. Instead of basil you can try different herbs, such as chives, coriander, parsley, oregano or tarragon. Serve with a salsa of freshly diced tomatoes and spring onions on the side.

8 flour tortillas
150g soft goat's cheese
2 tablespoons chopped fresh basil
Maldon salt
freshly ground black pepper
extra virgin olive oil

Preheat the grill to high. Lay three of the tortillas on a flat work surface and spread or crumble the goat's cheese evenly over them. Sprinkle over the basil and season with salt and pepper. Place the other tortillas on top. Brush with olive oil and sprinkle with a little more salt.

Transfer to one or two baking trays and grill for about 2 minutes. Turn the quesadillas over, brush with oil and grill for a further 2 minutes. Cut into wedges and serve immediately.

Pitta stuffed with Greek yogurt, feta & cucumber

SERVES 2 / PREP TIME: 7 MINUTES / COOKING TIME: 2-3 MINUTES

To me pitta bread always looks like oven mitts and has no character or charm whatsoever. But warm it up a little, gently prise it apart to make a pouch and fill it with something delicious and it can be heavenly. I like the fact that knives and forks are abandoned in this type of eating – it's messy food, so it's impossible to get away with a clean chin. It's also food you don't have to sit around a table to eat, but do make sure that a large napkin is at hand. Go for a bottle of retsina, a Greek wine with a distinctive flavour and aroma that comes from the pine resin added to it.

2–4 pitta breads
225g Greek yogurt
100g Greek feta cheese, crumbled
1/2 cucumber, peeled and diced
a few fresh mint leaves, finely chopped
a handful of fresh chives, finely chopped
2 teaspoons extra virgin olive oil
Maldon salt
freshly ground black pepper

Preheat the oven to warm and put in the pitta breads to heat up (don't have the oven too hot, otherwise the pitta breads will get hard and crisp).

Meanwhile, in a bowl, mix the yogurt with the feta. Stir in the cucumber, herbs and olive oil, and season well with salt and pepper. Gently make the breads into pouches, spoon in the filling and eat immediately.

Welsh rarebit

SERVES 1–2 / PREP TIME: 10 MINUTES / COOKING TIME: 5 MINUTES

When you don't want your supper to be an event, Welsh Rarebit will fit the bill – it's food with its sleeves rolled up. Every time I eat this I am always amazed that I don't make it more often, so I suggest buying extra ingredients as I am sure you will want to make seconds. Have a few fresh green salad leaves, such as butter or romaine lettuce, on the side, and if you want to go a step further make some fresh warm apple sauce.

140g Cheddar cheese, grated
60g unsalted butter, melted, plus extra for buttering toast
1/2 teaspoon English mustard powder
4 teaspoons cider or beer
2 teaspoons Worcestershire sauce
1 medium egg yolk
Maldon salt
freshly ground black pepper
2 slices of white bread, crusts off

Preheat the grill to high. Put the grated cheese, melted butter, mustard, cider or beer, Worcestershire sauce and egg yolk in a mixing bowl. Mix together well and season generously with salt and pepper.

Toast the bread very lightly and butter one side. Pile the cheese mixture on the buttered side, piling it up and reaching to the edges. Put on a baking sheet and grill until the cheese becomes bubbly and brown. Serve immediately.

Fried halloumi with capers, sun-blushed tomatoes, basil & chives

SERVES 2 / PREP TIME: 5 MINUTES / COOKING TIME: 5 MINUTES

Halloumi is a Middle Eastern sheep's milk cheese. It comes in blocks and is delicious fried in olive oil. To enjoy it at its best, eat it as soon as it comes from the pan. If you leave it to cool for 5 or 10 minutes it will become a little rubbery and lose a lot of its palatability. For this simple dish fried halloumi is partnered with sweet and juicy sun-blushed tomatoes (do use the oil they come in for the dressing). A baguette will go nicely with this. In fact, it's quite enjoyable to layer the halloumi and the rest of the trimmings on to the bread and wolf it down.

175g halloumi cheese
extra virgin olive oil
a few leaves of fresh basil, torn
2 heaped tablespoons roughly chopped sun-blushed tomatoes
2 teaspoons capers
1 tablespoon chopped fresh chives
Maldon salt
freshly ground black pepper
a couple of caper berries for garnishing

Cut the halloumi into slices as thick as a £2 coin. Coat the bottom of a heavy-based frying pan generously with olive oil. When the oil starts to shimmer, add the halloumi slices. Keep a watchful eye as they brown quite quickly. Once they are golden and toasty, turn them over and cook the other side. When they are ready, remove them to kitchen paper to absorb any extra oil.

Put the halloumi in a dish with the basil, tomatoes, capers and chives. Add another swirl of olive oil (or oil from the tomatoes) and season well with salt and pepper. Garnish with a couple of caper berries and serve immediately.

Another idea: Halloumi with pine nuts, mint & caper berries

In a mixing bowl, mix together 2 tablespoons of white wine vinegar and 1/2 teaspoon of caster sugar. Add a handful of finely chopped fresh mint leaves and leave for a few minutes. Add 3 tablespoons of extra virgin olive oil, mixing well, then add 2 chopped caper berries, 2 teaspoons of pine nuts and a handful of rocket. Toss so all the ingredients are well coated, and season well. Cook the halloumi as above and, when golden and crisp, place it on top of the salad.

Crab dressed with tarragon & mustard with sourdough toast

SERVES 1-2 / PREP TIME: 10 MINUTES

Fresh crab can be good, but adding a few key ingredients will make it really delicious. As there are very few ingredients in this dish, it is essential that every one of them is excellent. The crab must be really fresh, so always buy from a reputable fishmonger. And make an effort to find a good bakery for the sourdough bread. There's nothing worse than bread that's a little tired – it's like sawing wood to get into it. Beurre de Baratte, an unsalted butter from Normandy, is heavenly on the bread. If you make a bit of effort when shopping, every mouthful of this dish will be a wonderful experience. A fine wine to have with this is a chilled Chablis.

160g fresh crabmeat
1 teaspoon Dijon mustard
a few sprigs of fresh tarragon, leaves only
juice of 1/2 lemon
Maldon salt
freshly ground black pepper
2 slices of sourdough bread
unsalted butter
watercress (optional)

In a bowl, mix the crabmeat with the mustard, tarragon leaves, lemon juice, and salt and pepper to taste.

Grill or toast the bread, spread with butter and top with the crabmeat. Eat immediately, perhaps with a few leaves of watercress on the side.

Pan-fried scallops with lemon zest, bay leaves & white peppercorns

SERVES 2 / PREP TIME: 8 MINUTES / COOKING TIME: 20 MINUTES

Pan-fried scallops are so easy and so delicious, but, like other types of seafood, they need to be cooked correctly. If they seem quite thick, I cut them in half, to be sure they cook evenly and won't be overcooked. Pounding the lemon zest in a mortar releases the oil from the skin – you'll be amazed how sweet the juice becomes. Pour the buttery juices from the scallops over the rice and have a little lamb's lettuce on the side.

220g short-grain Italian or Spanish white rice
grated zest of 1 lemon
1/2 teaspoon white peppercorns
Maldon salt
100g unsalted butter
4 fresh bay leaves
2–4 scallops, sliced in half horizontally if large
a few leaves of lamb's lettuce

Cook the rice as per the packet instructions. Meanwhile, pound the lemon zest and peppercorns with a pinch of salt in a mortar. You want the peppercorns to crack but not to be completely ground down.

Melt the butter in a small frying pan until sizzling. Add the lemon zest mixture and the bay leaves. When the mixture is sizzling and spitting, toss in the scallops, giving each one its own space. Cook them for about 3 minutes, turning them over halfway.

Put the scallops on plates with the rice and pour over the buttery juices from the pan. Add some lamb's lettuce to the plates and serve immediately.

Spaghetti with crab & thyme

SERVES 2 / PREP TIME: 10 MINUTES / COOKING TIME: 8-12 MINUTES

This is a fairly rich dish so only a small amount of pasta and crabmeat should be needed. I prefer white crabmeat to the brown and it must be as fresh as possible. The thyme brings an earthy quality to the crab and with perfectly al dente spaghetti you'll have a refined dish. I first had this combination in Italy, served with prosecco, an Italian sparkling wine.

175g spaghetti
125g fresh white crabmeat
juice of 1/2 lemon
1 spring onion, finely chopped
a few sprigs of fresh thyme, leaves only
Maldon salt
freshly ground black pepper
2 teaspoons Tuscan extra virgin olive oil

Cook the spaghetti according to the packet instructions in plenty of boiling salted water until al dente; drain and return to the saucepan.

While the spaghetti is cooking, put the crabmeat in a bowl and break it up with a fork, then add the lemon juice, spring onion and thyme. Season generously with salt and pepper.

Add the crab mixture to the hot pasta and drizzle over the olive oil. Check the seasoning and serve immediately.

Another idea: Penne with lemon, garlic, goat's cheese & basil

Cook 200g penne in a large pan of boiling salted water, as per the packet instructions, until al dente. Meanwhile, drizzle a little extra virgin olive oil into a frying pan and heat, then add 2 cloves of garlic, sliced, and the grated zest of 2 lemons, and cook for about 3 minutes. Turn into a serving bowl and add 75g pitted black olives and 160g soft goat's cheese, cut into cubes. Mix 1 tablespoon lemon juice with 3 tablespoons extra virgin olive oil and spoon over.

Drain the penne, add to the bowl and toss together. Season well with salt and pepper, then scatter over a handful of basil leaves and serve immediately.

Steamed Dover sole with hot ginger oil

SERVES 2 / PREP TIME: 10 MINUTES / COOKING TIME: 5 MINUTES

In Asian cooking hot oil is often poured on to vegetables and herbs, rather than the vegetables being cooked in the oil. I've adapted that idea for this recipe. I find the key here is to be very generous with the spring onion and ginger, and to also use the green part of the spring onion, which we tend to discard in Western cooking. Serve this dish with Thai white rice.

2 Dover sole fillets
4cm piece of fresh ginger, cut into fine strips
4 spring onions, finely sliced diagonally
4 tablespoons groundnut oil
2 lime wedges

Bring a large pan of water to the boil. Set a steamer or colander on top and lay the sole fillets in the steamer. Cover and steam until cooked: this should only take a few minutes.

Meanwhile, put the ginger and spring onions in a heatproof bowl. Heat the groundnut oil in a frying pan until it begins to smoke. Pour the hot oil over the onions and ginger and let it sit for a couple of minutes.

Place the fish on serving plates and spoon over the ginger and spring onion oil. Serve with the lime wedges.

Grilled salmon fillet with lemon & cress

SERVES 2 / PREP TIME: 10 MINUTES / COOKING TIME: 5–7 MINUTES

Grilled salmon has quite a delicate flavour. Sprinkling fresh cress on top adds a gentle fiery kick. Serve this with new potatoes – when they are in season, hunt out the tiny Jersey ones for the best flavour. For a change from butter, pour some French dressing over the potatoes and scatter over some chopped fresh basil, chives or parsley.

340g piece of wild salmon or organic salmon fillet, cut in half
extra virgin olive oil
juice of 1 lemon
Maldon salt
2 small handfuls of cress

Preheat the grill to high. Place the salmon on a baking tray and drizzle over some olive oil and half of the lemon juice. Season generously with salt. Place under the grill and cook for 5–7 minutes or until the flesh has turned pale and opaque and the flakes of flesh will separate.

Remove the fish and place on a serving plate. Squeeze over the rest of the lemon juice, add another drizzle of olive oil and finish each serving with a handful of cress. Serve immediately.

Smoked sea trout with a salad of chicory, grapes, chives & mangetout with a warm walnut dressing

SERVES 2 / PREP TIME: 15 MINUTES / COOKING TIME: 5 MINUTES

A warm vinaigrette does wonders to a salad, enhancing all the flavours of the various ingredients. If you can't find smoked trout, smoked salmon would make a very good substitute, as it goes equally well with this tasty combination. If you are using smoked salmon, cut it into strips.

2 smoked sea trout fillets, skinned and flaked
1 head chicory, separated into leaves
6 mangetout, sliced
6 green grapes, cut in half and deseeded if necessary
2 teaspoons roughly chopped walnuts
a small bunch of fresh chives, snipped

Dressing
2 tablespoons walnut oil
1 teaspoon runny honey
1 teaspoon lemon juice
Maldon salt
freshly ground black pepper

Put the fish, chicory, mangetout, grapes, walnuts and chives in a serving dish.

In a saucepan, whisk together the ingredients for the dressing, then gently warm through. Whisk once again, then pour over the salad. Toss the salad and serve immediately.

Seared halibut steaks brushed with a lemon & coriander dressing

SERVES 2 / PREP TIME: 10 MINUTES / COOKING TIME: 4-6 MINUTES

If you're cooking this in the summer, get out the barbecue and pop the halibut steaks on the grill for a Saturday supper or Sunday brunch. Serve them with a warm salad of potatoes and green beans dressed with chives and extra virgin olive oil, and a fresh New World white wine from South Africa, Australia or California.

Dressing

3 tablespoons extra virgin olive oil
2 teaspoons lemon juice
1/2 teaspoon caster sugar
Maldon salt
freshly ground black pepper

2 halibut steaks, about 200g each
a small bunch of fresh coriander, finely chopped
grated zest of 1/2 lemon

Preheat the grill to high. In a bowl, mix the olive oil with the lemon juice, sugar, and salt and pepper to taste. Brush this dressing over the fish, then grill for 2–3 minutes on each side or until cooked. Alternatively, cook in a frying pan over a high heat. Test with a fork – if the fish is soft, it's ready.

Let it rest for a few minutes, then brush it with more of the dressing, sprinkle with the coriander and lemon zest, and serve.

Another idea: Haddock fillets with herb butter

Herb butter can be made in advance and is delicious with fish or meat. Pulse the following in a food processor until a smooth paste forms (this makes 4–6 servings): 150g unsalted butter, 3 anchovy fillets, 1 teaspoon of grated lemon zest, 1 clove of garlic, crushed, 3 tablespoons of chopped chives, a handful of fresh flat-leaf parsley leaves, 2 teaspoons of capers, rinsed and drained, and a pinch of freshly ground black pepper. Lay a sheet of cling film on the work surface and spoon on the herb butter in a line. Roll it up to form a log and refrigerate.

Coat the bottom of a large frying pan with a thin layer of olive oil. When the oil is hot, cook the haddock fillets for 2–3 minutes on each side or until the flesh will just flake. Sprinkle with salt. Make a bed of watercress on each plate, set a haddock fillet on top and add a few slices of the herb butter.

Sea bass with parsley & caper berry salsa

SERVES 2 / PREP TIME: 14 MINUTES / COOKING TIME: 5 MINUTES

Sea bass is a fine-flavoured fish and it works well with this slightly tart salsa. Delicious vegetables to have on the side are buttery boiled potatoes and, if you can source them, Kenyan green beans. A fine glass of Sauvignon Blanc would be a sound choice to accompany this dish.

extra virgin olive oil for frying the fish
2 sea bass fillets
2 teaspoons finely chopped fresh flat-leaf parsley
2 lemon wedges

Salsa
1 teaspoon crushed green peppercorns
4 caper berries, finely chopped
a few sprigs of fresh dill, finely chopped
1 small shallot, finely chopped
2 teaspoons extra virgin olive oil
Maldon salt
freshly ground black pepper

In a little bowl, mix together all of the ingredients for the salsa. Season to taste with salt and pepper, then set aside.

Drizzle some olive oil over the bottom of a heavy-based frying pan. When the oil is hot, add the sea bass, skin side down, and cook for about 3 minutes. Turn the fillets over and cook for a further 2 minutes. Season the fish and sprinkle with the parsley, then serve with the salsa and lemon wedges.

Stir-fried chicken with ginger, yellow tomatoes, mangetout, spring onions & coriander

SERVES 1–2 / PREP TIME: 7 MINUTES / COOKING TIME: 8 MINUTES

In the summer months yellow tomatoes appear in the markets and shops. They don't taste hugely different from red tomatoes – perhaps a little less acidic and softer – but they are the prettiest colour. The colour of food is very important. It's like the paint on an artist's palette. If food looks beautiful it lures you in with anticipation of what is to be tasted.

extra virgin olive oil
400g boneless chicken strips
4 yellow tomatoes, roughly chopped
4 spring onions, shredded
Maldon salt
2 teaspoons grated fresh ginger
175g mangetout, cut in half lengthways
freshly ground black pepper
a handful of fresh coriander leaves, roughly chopped

Heat a swirl of olive oil in a large frying pan over a high heat. When it is hot, brown the chicken strips all over. Add the tomatoes, spring onions and a liberal pinch of salt. Cook for a few minutes until the tomatoes are soft and mushy. Add the ginger and mangetout and cook, stirring, for a further few minutes until the mangetout are cooked but still retain their crunchiness. Season to taste with salt and pepper, scatter over the coriander and serve.

Pork fillets with celery salt & green peppercorns

SERVES 2 / PREP TIME: 10 MINUTES / COOKING TIME: 10 MINUTES

This celery salt and green peppercorn butter would work just as well with chicken, or mix in some chopped parsley and serve it with fish. Accompany the pork with a round lettuce salad drizzled with a little extra virgin olive oil and lemon juice.

4 teaspoons celery seeds
1/2 teaspoon green peppercorns
Maldon salt
150g unsalted butter
2 pork fillets (tenderloin), about 170g each

Crush the celery seeds in a mortar with a pestle. When pounded add the peppercorns and a generous pinch of salt.

Heat 50g of the butter in a heavy-based frying pan. When the butter stops frothing fry the pork fillets for 7–8 minutes, turning to cook all sides. Remove to a warm serving dish.

Discard the butter and wipe out the frying pan. Melt the remaining butter, then skim off any froth. Stir in the celery and peppercorn mixture and cook for a couple of minutes. Pour over the pork fillets and serve immediately.

Another idea: Calf's kidney with shallots, Marsala & tarragon

I don't often eat kidneys, but they make a very tasty dish and aren't difficult to prepare or cook. Rinse and pat dry 250g fresh calf's kidneys, then remove any white membrane, veins and ducts. Season with salt and pepper, then dust with plain flour. In a frying pan, heat 1 tablespoon of olive oil with 25g unsalted butter. Sauté the kidneys for about 2 minutes on each side or until browned but pink on the inside. Remove the kidneys to a plate and cover to keep warm.

Finely chop 1 large shallot and sauté in the pan until soft. Add 2 tablespoons of Marsala wine and 1 tablespoon of crème fraîche and simmer until the sauce has reduced by about one-third. Stir in a few fresh tarragon leaves and season to taste with salt and freshly ground black pepper. Pour the sauce over the kidneys and serve with a green salad.

Asparagus with hollandaise sauce

SERVES 2 / PREP TIME: 5 MINUTES / COOKING TIME: 10 MINUTES

Asparagus with hollandaise is a classic dish that is hard to beat as it is so utterly delicious. Make this during the English asparagus season and serve it with some really good ham, such as French jambon de Bayonne or air-cured Italian San Daniele, and open a chilled bottle of Frascati. Without the ham, asparagus with hollandaise could be served as a simple starter or snack.

3 medium egg yolks
225g unsalted butter, melted
a squeeze of lemon juice
Maldon salt
freshly ground black pepper
2 bunches of asparagus
Bayonne or San Daniele ham, to serve

Set a heatproof bowl over a pan of water on a moderate heat. Put the egg yolks in the bowl and add a splash of water. Gently whisk for a few seconds. Very slowly add the melted butter, whisking constantly until thick and light. Whisk in the lemon juice and season with salt and pepper.

Steam the asparagus until it is al dente, then serve with the hollandaise sauce and slices of ham.

mono

Sliced fillet steak with anchovy & basil butter on toast

SERVES 2 / PREP TIME: 10 MINUTES / COOKING TIME: 8 MINUTES

This open sandwich is totally delicious. The flavoured butter is quite subtle, with hints of basil amidst the salty taste of anchovies, and the lovely tender texture of the steak contrasts with the crispiness of the toast. I find it a perfect dish. It has the convenience of a snack but the satisfaction of a meal.

4 anchovy fillets
50g unsalted butter, at room temperature, plus extra for frying steak
1 spring onion, finely chopped
4 large fresh basil leaves, torn
Maldon salt
400g fillet steak
4 slices of white country bread, crusts removed
freshly ground black pepper

Pound the anchovies in a mortar with a pestle, then add the butter, spring onion, basil leaves and a pinch of salt. Continue pounding until you have a creamy paste.

With a rolling pin or pestle, pound the steak to make it thinner. Heat a knob of butter in a frying pan. When it sizzles and turns brown add the steak and cook for 2–3 minutes on each side, depending on how rare you like it. Remove the steak and cut it into strips.

While the steak is cooking, toast the bread and spread with the anchovy butter. Add the sliced steak, sprinkle with salt and pepper and eat immediately.

Another idea: Grilled fillet steak with a red salsa & horseradish vinaigrette

Preheat the grill to high. For the salad, combine 5 small cooked beetroots, peeled and sliced, 1 radicchio and 1 chicory, shredded, and a few leaves of purple basil in a salad bowl. In a small bowl, whisk together 1 tablespoon of red wine vinegar, 2 teaspoons of creamed horseradish, 3 tablespoons of extra virgin olive oil and salt to taste. Pour over the salad and give it a good toss.

Whack the steak on both sides, then rub with a little olive oil. Grill for 3–5 minutes on each side, if you like it rare; 5–7 minutes if you prefer it medium rare. Sprinkle with salt and slice. Add to the salad or serve alongside.

Lamb, thyme & garlic brochettes

SERVES 2 / PREP TIME: 10 MINUTES / COOKING TIME: 10 MINUTES

These brochettes can be cooked on the grill or, in summer, on the barbecue. When done correctly, barbecued food can be delicious. You only need to follow a few basic rules and you're in clover. The key is low, even heat and lots of fragrant wood smoke – cooking can only begin once the charcoal is completely covered in grey ash and no red glow is visible. The heat is right when you can hold your hand 12cm above the fire for 5 seconds. Serve these brochettes with a salad of crumbled feta cheese, sliced tomatoes and a generous quantity of roughly chopped fresh flat-leaf parsley, all drizzled with extra virgin olive oil, salt and pepper.

500g boned shoulder of lamb, cut into cubes
2 small to medium red onions, cut into wedges
extra virgin olive oil
a few sprigs of fresh thyme, leaves only
3 garlic cloves, finely chopped
Maldon salt

Thread the lamb and onions alternately on to soaked wooden satay sticks. Lay the brochettes in a dish. Drizzle over some olive oil and sprinkle with the thyme leaves, garlic and salt.

Preheat the barbecue (or the grill). Cook the brochettes for 7–10 minutes, turning as appropriate. Serve with a feta salad.

two

feeling virtuous – light and healthy dishes

Grilled prawns with avocado, tomato & coriander salad

SERVES 2 / PREP TIME: 20 MINUTES / COOKING TIME: 4 MINUTES

For this recipe you need big prawns, such as Mediterranean prawns. You could also use tiger prawns but double the grilling time. Serve with wedges of lemon and really fresh, crusty baguette, plus a glass of chilled Chablis to sip slowly.

4–6 large raw prawns
juice of 1/2 lemon
2 tablespoons extra virgin olive oil, plus extra for brushing prawns
Maldon salt
freshly ground black pepper
1 avocado, stoned, peeled and diced
2 ripe tomatoes, peeled, deseeded and diced
a small bunch of fresh coriander, leaves only, finely chopped
a few fresh chives, snipped
2 lemon wedges

Preheat the grill to high. Peel the prawns, leaving on the last tail section if you like. To butterfly the prawns, cut along the curved back of each one to split it open, without cutting all the way through. Open up the prawns flat and remove the vein.

In a large bowl, whisk the lemon juice with the olive oil and season to taste with salt and pepper. Add the avocado, tomatoes and coriander and toss gently in the dressing.

Place the prawns on a grill pan, brush them with olive oil and season with salt. Put them under the grill and cook for 2–3 minutes on each side. Sprinkle the prawns with the chives and serve with the avocado salad and lemon wedges to squeeze over.

Lychee, mint, coriander & prawn salad with a chilli dressing

SERVES 2 / PREP TIME: 15 MINUTES

Lychees are the fruit of a large evergreen tree. They have been cultivated in China since the 1st century BC. The fruit was considered such a fine delicacy that the Imperial court would dispatch swift horses to the north of Canton to bring them back to the palace. They are even reputed to have brought down an Emperor, as his lover's great passion for lychees stretched the court financially.

225g lychees, peeled and stoned
2 spring onions, finely chopped
75g cooked peeled prawns, cut into small chunks
a small bunch of fresh coriander, leaves only
a small bunch of fresh mint, leaves only
a handful of lamb's lettuce

Chilli dressing
1/2 red chilli, deseeded and finely chopped
1 garlic clove, finely chopped
8 teaspoons extra virgin olive oil
grated zest of 1 lime
2 teaspoons lime juice
1 teaspoon caster sugar
Maldon salt
freshly ground black pepper

To make the dressing, combine the chilli, garlic, olive oil, lime zest and juice, sugar, and some salt and pepper in a salad bowl. Mix together well. Add the lychees, spring onions and prawns, and spoon the dressing over the ingredients. Add the coriander, mint and lamb's lettuce. Toss well, then check the seasoning and serve immediately.

Papaya salad with lime chicken breasts

SERVES 2 / PREP TIME: 15 MINUTES / COOKING TIME: 20 MINUTES

Papaya is rich in beneficial beta-carotene, and is thought to be a great healer of upset stomachs. It's a very sweet fruit, which is why it is often combined with the aromatic sharpness of lime. If you don't feel like eating chicken, try grilled prawns or fresh tuna steaks with the papaya salad.

2 chicken breasts
extra virgin olive oil
grated zest and juice of 2 limes
Maldon salt
1 red onion, finely chopped
1 garlic clove, crushed
1 tablespoon fish sauce
2 teaspoons caster sugar
1 Cos lettuce
1 small ripe papaya, peeled and diced
a bunch of fresh mint, leaves only, finely chopped
2 lime wedges

Preheat the oven to 200°C/gas 6. Place the chicken in a small roasting tin. Brush with olive oil and sprinkle with half the lime juice and a little salt. Roast for 20 minutes or until golden and cooked through.

Meanwhile, heat a little olive oil in a frying pan and sauté the onion and garlic until soft. Transfer to a serving bowl and add the remaining lime juice, the lime zest, fish sauce and sugar. Toss the lettuce leaves in the dressing, then add the papaya and mint leaves. Serve immediately with the chicken and lime wedges.

Pan-fried mackerel with a cucumber & dill salad

SERVES 2 / PREP TIME: 10 MINUTES / COOKING TIME: 6 MINUTES

Mackerel is a fish that we are encouraged to eat as it's rich in essential fatty acids. It has a very distinctive taste that works well with a little cucumber and dill salad, in a delicious Nordic fashion. Buttery boiled potatoes would go perfectly with this dish and perhaps a Riesling Kabinett from the Mosel-Saar-Ruwer district in Germany. What more could you want?

4 teaspoons extra virgin olive oil, plus extra for frying fish
2 teaspoons white wine vinegar
1 teaspoon Dijon mustard
1½ teaspoons caster sugar
Maldon salt
freshly ground black pepper
400g cucumber
a handful of fresh dill, roughly chopped
2 mackerel fillets

In a medium bowl, whisk together the olive oil, vinegar, mustard, sugar, and salt and pepper to taste. Peel the cucumber, cut it lengthways in half and use a teaspoon to scoop out the seeds. Slice the cucumber halves and add to the dressing. Scatter over the dill.

Drizzle a little olive oil into a frying pan. When the oil is hot, fry the mackerel fillets for about 3 minutes on each side or until the flesh will just flake. Remove to plates, season and serve immediately with the salad.

Squid, mint & pine nut salad

SERVES 2 / PREP TIME: 15 MINUTES PLUS AT LEAST 30 MINUTES MARINATING

COOKING TIME: 3 MINUTES

Warm salads are perfect when you need a bit of heat in your food but you also crave some fresh ingredients. I love the combination of cold ingredients with warm ones. The only downside of this is that you cannot let the food hang around as the lettuce will go limp and soggy. So eat pronto.

250g squid, bodies cut into rings, tentacles left whole
3 tablespoons extra virgin olive oil
1/2 red chilli, deseeded and finely chopped
grated zest and juice of 1 lime
1 garlic clove, crushed
1/2 teaspoon caster sugar
Maldon salt
a small bunch of fresh mint, finely chopped
a handful of rocket
50g pine nuts

In a bowl, mix together the squid, olive oil, chilli, lime zest and garlic. Toss well so that the squid pieces are thoroughly coated. Allow to marinate for 30 minutes to 1 hour.

Whisk together the lime juice, sugar and some salt in a salad bowl. Heat a heavy-based frying pan on a high heat, then add the squid and let it sear for 1–2 minutes. Pour over the squid marinade and let it bubble and hiss for about 30 seconds.

Tip the squid into the salad bowl, mix in the mint, rocket and pine nuts, and serve immediately.

Salmon with pink peppercorns, chervil, crème fraîche & Puy lentils

SERVES 2 / PREP TIME: 7 MINUTES / COOKING TIME: 20 MINUTES

If you can find it, use wild salmon for this recipe. A couple of fillets are not going to break the bank, but they are going to leave you licking your chops and rubbing your belly afterwards. Organic salmon is the next choice. Pink peppercorns have a delightful flavour, albeit a little perfumed. Lacy chervil is subtle and delicate – I'd certainly put both these ingredients into the more female camp of food. The earthy flavour of Puy lentils perfectly complements the fish.

200g Puy lentils
Maldon salt
freshly ground black pepper
extra virgin olive oil
2 pieces of salmon fillet, about 200g each
a knob of unsalted butter
4 shallots, finely chopped
1 teaspoon pink peppercorns
2 teaspoons crème fraîche
a handful of fresh chervil, finely chopped

Preheat the oven to 170°C/gas 3. Cook the lentils as per the packet instructions. When ready, put them to one side. Before serving, season the lentils well with salt and pepper and drizzle over some of your finest extra virgin olive oil.

While the lentils are cooking, put the salmon in a roasting dish, pour over a conservative swirl of olive oil and add a good sprinkling of salt. Bake the salmon for about 10 minutes or until the flesh has turned pale pink.

Meanwhile, gently melt the butter in a small pan and sauté the shallots until soft, but retaining a little crunch. Add the pink peppercorns and stir in the crème fraîche, then throw in the chervil and a little pinch of salt. Cook for enough time to warm it through.

Remove the salmon to two serving plates. Place the pink peppercorn mixture on top of the salmon and the lentils on the side. Eat immediately.

Steamed lemon sole with lemon zest, capers & mint

SERVES 2 / PREP TIME: 10 MINUTES / COOKING TIME: ABOUT 3 MINUTES

I love using my bamboo steamer – it cooks food incredibly quickly and I like the woody smell it gives out while it's being used. These steamers are available from most Asian supermarkets. The alternative for this easy-peasy fish dinner is to use an ordinary steamer or a covered colander set over a saucepan. You can also cook other fish this way, cod for example, which would take about 5–7 minutes to steam. I like to add a tiny amount of capers, as they are a sudden little surprise when your tastebuds run into them. With the fish I'd serve mashed potatoes seasoned with lashings of black pepper.

4 teaspoons finely chopped fresh mint
2 teaspoons capers, rinsed and drained
2 teaspoons finely grated lemon zest
1 tablespoon extra virgin olive oil
Maldon salt
freshly ground black pepper
2 fillets of lemon sole, about 170g each, skin removed
2 lemon wedges

Put all of the ingredients, except the fish and lemon wedges, into a bowl and mix them together.

Bring a pan of water to the boil. Line a bamboo steamer basket with baking parchment. Lay the fish on the paper and spoon over the herb mixture. Cover the steamer, set it over the boiling water and steam for about 3 minutes or until the fish is cooked through (test with a fork: if the fish is soft, it's ready). Remove and serve with the lemon wedges.

Swordfish with sweet & sour peppers & basil

SERVES 2 / PREP TIME: 10 MINUTES / COOKING TIME: 30 MINUTES

Swordfish steaks are quite macho, so I don't feel it's necessary to add endless accoutrements, but these sweet and sour peppers will really make your tastebuds zing. A little portion of Thai rice on the side would be delicious. Or have jacket-baked potatoes and put the peppers on top of the cut potato with a little crème fraîche.

1 red pepper, cut into medium shreds
1 red onion, roughly chopped
2 teaspoons muscovado sugar
4 teaspoons balsamic vinegar
Maldon salt
2 swordfish steaks
extra virgin olive oil
freshly ground black pepper
a handful of fresh basil leaves

Preheat the oven to 190°C/gas 5. Combine the red pepper and onion in an ovenproof dish. Sprinkle with the sugar and then with the balsamic vinegar and a hearty pinch of salt. Mix together well. Cover with aluminium foil and place in the oven. Cook for about 30 minutes or until tender.

Towards the end of this time, heat a ridged cast-iron grill pan. When it is hot, rub the swordfish steaks with a little olive oil, season well with salt and pepper and place in the pan. Char-grill for 4–5 minutes on each side, according to how thick the steaks are. Scatter the basil leaves over the peppers and serve them with the fish.

Grilled red mullet with oven-dried tomatoes & two-coloured basil

SERVES 4–6 / PREP TIME: 25 MINUTES / COOKING TIME: ABOUT 2 HOURS

Hunt down small red mullet (called rouget in France) and ask your fishmonger to gut them and remove the scales. To make this dish really colourful, look for yellow and red tomatoes or even green ones. Do the same with basil, finding some red as well as green if you can. If you're in a hurry, you can prepare the tomatoes in advance.

7 small tomatoes in assorted colours
1/2 teaspoon caster sugar
Maldon salt
a few sprigs of fresh thyme, leaves only
extra virgin olive oil
a small handful of black Provençal olives, pitted and finely chopped
2 small red mullet, cleaned and scaled
a small bunch of fresh basil, preferably mixed red and green, shredded

Preheat the oven to its lowest setting. Cut out the core from the tomatoes, then cut them in half and remove all the insides. Place the tomato shells on a baking tray. Sprinkle with the sugar, a pinch of salt and the thyme leaves. Drizzle over olive oil sparingly. Place in the oven and cook for about 2 hours or until the tomatoes are dried out. Finely chop the tomatoes and mix with the olives, a little more olive oil and a pinch of salt.

Preheat the grill to high. Place the red mullet on a grill pan, brush with olive oil and sprinkle with a little salt. Grill for about 3 minutes or until the fish are cooked. Test with a fork: if soft they are cooked. Take care not to overcook.

Put the fish on plates, top each with a spoonful of the tomato and olive mixture and sprinkle over the basil. Serve immediately.

Fillets of tuna with borlotti beans with tomato, parsley & chives

SERVES 2 / PREP TIME: 15 MINUTES / COOKING TIME: 25 MINUTES

Canned tuna fillets (Ortiz is the brand to look for) have a delicious creamy taste – they literally melt in your mouth. Ordinary canned tuna doesn't come close in either looks or taste. When you have time, buy dry borlotti beans, soak them overnight, then simmer until tender. Canned beans are a convenient alternative, but be sure to rinse and drain them well. If you prefer a spicier dish, add more chilli flakes; alternatively, reduce the amount of chilli if it is not to your liking.

extra virgin olive oil
1/2 onion, finely chopped
2 garlic cloves, finely chopped
2 tablespoons tomato purée
a pinch of chilli flakes
2 small vine-ripened tomatoes, peeled, deseeded and chopped
400g can borlotti beans, rinsed and drained
125ml water
a small bunch of fresh flat-leaf parsley, finely chopped
Maldon salt
freshly ground black pepper
a few fresh chives, finely chopped
250g can tuna fillets, drained

Coat the bottom of a heavy-based saucepan thinly with olive oil. Add the onion and garlic and cook over a moderate heat until soft. Add the tomato purée and cook for about 2 minutes, stirring to integrate well with the onions and garlic. Add the chilli flakes, tomatoes, beans and water. Bring to simmering point, then cook for about 20 minutes or until the sauce has thickened.

Stir in the parsley and season to taste with salt and pepper. Transfer to a hot serving dish, sprinkle over the chives and lay the tuna fillets over the top. Serve immediately.

Lime-baked tuna with basil potatoes

SERVES 2 / PREP TIME: 5 MINUTES / COOKING TIME: 20 MINUTES

The leaves from the kaffir lime tree, which have a divine limey-lemony fragrance, are often used in Asian cooking. You can find them, both fresh and frozen, in oriental food shops as well as some supermarkets. When buying the tuna for this dish, go for a thin slice rather than a chunkier one. If your potatoes are fresh and young, leave the skins on, as they impart a nice earthy flavour.

8 new potatoes, washed
extra virgin olive oil
Maldon salt
2 pieces of tuna fillet, about 200g each
grated zest and juice of 1 lime
8 kaffir lime leaves, finely shredded
a small bunch of fresh basil, leaves only, torn
1 teaspoon pink peppercorns, crushed

Preheat the oven to 180°C/gas 4. Cook the potatoes in plenty of boiling salted water for about 20 minutes or until tender when pricked with a fork. Drain, then slash with a knife. Tip into a bowl and add a liberal amount of olive oil and a large pinch of salt. Cover to keep warm.

While the potatoes are cooking, lay the tuna fillets in a roasting dish and drizzle over 2 teaspoons of olive oil. Add the lime juice, then the zest and a pinch of salt. Place the shredded lime leaves on top of the tuna. Bake for 10–15 minutes, depending on how well cooked you like it.

Transfer the tuna with its juices to a hot serving dish. Add the basil leaves and peppercorns to the potatoes and serve immediately.

Baked trout with cherry tomatoes & turmeric

SERVES 2 / PREP TIME: 15 MINUTES / COOKING TIME: 10-12 MINUTES

Turmeric adds a lovely yellow colour to this sauce, which glows alongside the vibrant hue of the tomatoes. Not only will you have a yummy supper, but also all of the ingredients in this dish have wonderful healthy properties. Turmeric, for example, is a great liver cleanser and does wonders for the skin, while trout is rich in omega 3 fats that help lower blood pressure and tomatoes offer vitamin C, which helps protect against cancer.

2 trout, about 455g each, scaled and cleaned
1 large lemon, cut into 8–10 slices
extra virgin olive oil
Maldon salt
1 red onion, finely chopped
2 garlic cloves, finely chopped
14 cherry tomatoes, quartered
1 teaspoon turmeric
1 teaspoon sugar
freshly ground black pepper

Preheat the oven to 240°C/gas 9. Take a sharp knife and cut angled incisions along the sides of the fish. This will help the fish to cook more quickly and the seasonings to be absorbed. Put three to five slices of lemon in the incisions in each fish and brush the outsides with olive oil and sprinkle with salt. Place on a baking tray in the oven and cook for 10–12 minutes.

Meanwhile, coat the bottom of a large frying pan with olive oil. When hot, add the onion and garlic and sauté until soft. Add the tomatoes and remaining lemon slices and sprinkle in the turmeric. Simmer away gently until the tomatoes become pulpy and start to form a sauce. Sprinkle over the sugar and season well with salt and pepper, then cook for a few more minutes.

As soon as the fish is ready, serve it with the sauce.

Lamb broth with cavolo nero & white vegetables

SERVES 2 / PREP TIME: 12 MINUTES / COOKING TIME: 30 MINUTES

When the weather gets cold, lamb broth will warm the cockles of your heart. Any vegetables can be used. I've gone for white ones, but orange ones such as carrots, swede and pumpkin work well, too. If you have more time throw in a little bit of pearl barley when simmering the lamb and before adding the vegetables – this will add another hour to the cooking time. Cavolo nero is a black cabbage from Italy. If hard to source, you can use Savoy cabbage instead.

extra virgin olive oil
3 lamb loin chops
1 onion, finely chopped
2 garlic cloves, finely chopped
1 bay leaf
1 teaspoon redcurrant jelly
Maldon salt
2 parsnips, peeled and roughly chopped
1/2 celeriac, peeled and roughly chopped
3 cavolo nero leaves without stalk, shredded

Lightly coat the bottom of a flameproof casserole or heavy-based saucepan with olive oil. When the oil is hot, brown the lamb chops on both sides. Add the onion and sauté for a few minutes, then add the garlic and cook until both are soft. Pour in enough water to cover, and add the bay leaf, redcurrant jelly and a big pinch of salt. Simmer gently for 20 minutes.

Add the parsnips and celeriac and cook for a further 10 minutes. Remove the lamb chops, cut the meat off the bone and cut into small chunks. Put the lamb back in the pan. Add the cavolo nero and cook for a final 5 minutes. Season to taste with salt. Serve in soup bowls.

Fillet of beef with a herb & spice crust

SERVES 2 / PREP TIME: 20 MINUTES / COOKING TIME: 5 MINUTES

There are three things vital to this recipe. First, you need a very sharp knife. Second, you must trim off any excess fat or sinew from the beef, so that you have an incredibly lean, tender piece of beef. And third, the herbs have to be chopped as finely as you can get them. This recipe works equally well with fresh tuna loin. I recommend you have a glass of Côtes du Rhône with the beef.

1 tablespoon finely chopped garlic
1 tablespoon finely chopped fresh ginger
1 tablespoon finely chopped fresh coriander
1 tablespoon finely chopped fresh flat-leaf parsley
1 teaspoon crushed star anise
Maldon salt
1 piece of beef fillet, about 600g, trimmed of all fat and sinew
toasted sesame oil

In a small bowl, mix together the garlic, ginger, coriander, parsley, star anise and a pinch of a salt. Transfer this herb mixture to a shallow dish or plate and spread it out. Roll the beef in the mixture until completely crusted.

Drizzle a little sesame oil in a heavy-based frying pan and heat it, then add the beef. Fry on a high heat for about 5 minutes or until it is seared on all sides; it will be pink inside. Cut the beef into thin slices and fan out on hot plates. Serve with a green salad.

Grilled chicken with broad beans, lime zest & chive butter

SERVES 2 / PREP TIME: 10 MINUTES / COOKING TIME: 10 MINUTES

I must admit I'm potty about broad beans. When they are young and tender, as they are in early summer, I eat them with their husks. Later on in the season, I only eat the emerald-green inner beans. If your beans are larger you will want to slip them out of their skins after steaming. Broad beans and lime are not the most obvious of bedfellows, but in Mexico this is an everyday culinary combination. It's perfect with grilled chicken.

2 skinless, boneless chicken breasts
grated zest and juice of 2 limes
extra virgin olive oil
Maldon salt
600g young, tender broad beans, shelled
a large knob of unsalted butter
a small handful of fresh chives
freshly ground black pepper

Preheat the grill to moderately high. Place the chicken breasts on a grill pan, pour over the lime juice and add a generous drizzle of olive oil and a good pinch of salt. Grill for 10 minutes or until cooked through and the skin is browned and crisp.

Meanwhile, steam the broad beans until tender but retaining a crunch. Melt the butter in a small saucepan or frying pan. Snip in the chives and let them bubble for a few seconds.

When the chicken is ready transfer it to a serving dish with the juices. Spoon the broad beans around, pour over the chive butter and sprinkle over the lime zest. Season with salt and pepper and serve immediately.

Moorish poached chicken with carrots, cumin & coriander

SERVES 2 / PREP TIME: 20 MINUTES / COOKING TIME: 40 MINUTES

This dish has a Spanish-Moroccan influence. Try to find bunches of small carrots and cook them whole. If small carrots aren't available you can use diced large carrots. Serve with some Spanish Calasparra rice tinted with a little saffron or turmeric, or potatoes fried with onions and loads of garlic.

extra virgin olive oil
2 chicken breasts
5 shallots, roughly chopped
5 garlic cloves, finely chopped
4 teaspoons ground cumin
about 350ml water
1/2 teaspoon sugar
Maldon salt
a small bunch of baby carrots, trimmed and scrubbed
a handful of fresh coriander leaves, roughly chopped

Lightly coat the bottom of a flameproof casserole with olive oil. When the oil is hot, brown the chicken breasts on both sides. Add the shallots and garlic and sauté until soft. Mix in the cumin. Add enough water just to cover the chicken. Add the sugar and season with salt. Bring to simmering point, then cook, uncovered, for about 20 minutes.

Add the carrots and cook for a further 10 minutes or until they are tender but still retain some crunch. Scatter with the coriander and serve.

Chicken breasts stuffed with porcini mushrooms, leeks & marjoram

SERVES 2 / PREP TIME: 15 MINUTES / COOKING TIME: 15 MINUTES

This is an easy way to spruce up a plain old chicken breast and give you a tasty dinner. I've used fresh porcini mushrooms, but most mushrooms would work just as well. The key is to cut up all the ingredients really finely, as this will blend the flavours better. Serve with crushed boiled potatoes dressed with olive oil.

a large knob of butter
2 small spring leeks, finely chopped
2 fresh porcini mushrooms, finely chopped
a few fresh marjoram leaves, finely chopped
Maldon salt
freshly ground black pepper
2 skinless, boneless chicken breasts
extra virgin olive oil

Preheat the oven to 190°C/gas 5. Melt the butter in a saucepan and gently sauté the leeks and mushrooms with the marjoram until soft. Season with salt and pepper.

With a sharp knife cut a horizontal pocket in each chicken breast. Season the inside of the pocket with salt and pepper, then stuff in the leek mixture and press the pocket to close. Place the breasts in a roasting tin. Drizzle with olive oil and season with salt and pepper. Roast for about 15 minutes or until the chicken is golden and cooked through. If the stuffing begins to come out into the tin and burn, cover with kitchen foil.

Honey, star anise & cinnamon chicken

SERVES 2 / PREP TIME: 30 MINUTES / COOKING TIME: 35 MINUTES

When food arrives at the table in a paper parcel, I always feel as though I'm receiving a present. This dish is best served with fragrant Thai rice or jasmine rice sprinkled with fresh herbs, such as Thai basil, chives, parsley or coriander, plus a simply cooked green vegetable.

2 chicken breasts
1 tablespoon runny honey
2 tablespoons soy sauce
30g unsalted butter, melted
2 garlic cloves, crushed
4 star anise
1 cinnamon stick, broken in half
4 cardamom pods, bashed
a few sprigs of fresh coriander, leaves only, finely chopped
1/2 red chilli, deseeded and thinly sliced

Preheat the oven to 190°C/gas 5. Place each chicken breast on a sheet of baking parchment. Combine the honey, soy sauce and butter in a small bowl. Brush this mixture over the chicken. Add the garlic, star anise, cinnamon sticks and cardamom pods to the chicken breasts, dividing these ingredients evenly. Add a couple of slices of chilli, then bring up the sides of each sheet of paper and fold over to form a sealed parcel.

Transfer the parcels to a baking tray. Bake for 35 minutes or until the chicken is tender and cooked. Sprinkle with the coriander and the rest of the chilli, and serve immediately.

Another idea: Grilled chicken with mango & coconut chutney

Grill 2 chicken breasts, drizzled with extra virgin olive oil and the juice of 1 lime under a moderate grill for 15–20 minutes, turning halfway through the time.

Meanwhile, place 40g desiccated coconut, 1 teaspoon of grated fresh ginger and 1/2 chopped green chilli in a food processor and pulse to a fine paste. Transfer to a small bowl and stir in 1 teaspoon of lime juice, 4 tablespoons of plain yogurt and 1 mango, cut into cubes. In a small frying pan, heat 1 tablespoon of sunflower oil over a moderate heat. When the oil is hot add 1 teaspoon of mustard seeds and 2 small sprigs of curry leaves. When the mustard seeds begin to pop, remove from the heat and transfer to kitchen paper to drain off excess oil. Add the mustard seeds to the coconut mixture and garnish with the curry leaves and a few fresh coriander leaves. Serve with the grilled chicken.

China-spice beef with wilted spring onions & coriander

SERVES 2 / PREP TIME: 7 MINUTES / COOKING TIME: 20 MINUTES

China spice consists of eight spices – star anise, cassia, fennel, garlic, mustard, black pepper, ginger and lemon peel – ground together. It's available in jars on most spice racks (Hambledon Herbs make a very tasty organic version). I like to serve the beef and onions on top of the rice, either in a bowl or on a plate.

220g Thai or jasmine rice
220g rump steak, thinly sliced and then cut into strips
1/2 teaspoon China spice
Maldon salt
sunflower oil
2 garlic cloves, crushed
6 spring onions, split lengthways up into the green stalks
a small bunch of fresh coriander, leaves only, roughly chopped

Boil or steam the rice as per the packet instructions.

Meanwhile, toss the strips of beef with the China spice in a bowl. Season generously with salt.

Drizzle a little oil into a wok or frying pan and heat until it shimmers. Add the strips of beef and stir-fry over a high heat for 1–2 minutes. Turn down the heat, add the garlic and spring onions and cook for a further minute or so. The onions should retain their crunchiness and the stalks should still be green. Remove with a slotted spoon and pile on top of the rice. Season well with salt and scatter with the coriander.

Japanese beef with ginger marinade & chives

SERVES 2 / PREP TIME: 15 MINUTES PLUS AT LEAST 1 HOUR INFUSING

Dig out the chopsticks for this dish or acquire some from your local takeaway. This is ideal served with sushi rice, a green salad with a little bit of Japanese seaweed, and some warm sake. The longer you leave the marinade to infuse, the stronger the flavour will become.

juice of 1 lime
2 tablespoons runny honey
2 teaspoons soy sauce
2 teaspoons grated fresh ginger
8 long strips of beef sirloin, about 220g in total
2 tablespoons toasted sesame oil
a small bunch of fresh chives

In a small mixing bowl, combine the lime juice, honey, soy sauce and ginger. Leave to infuse for at least 1 hour.

Brush the strips of raw beef with the sesame oil. Lay them on two serving plates and fold each of them over into a small parcel. Remove the ginger from the marinade using a slotted spoon and place it on the plates with the beef. Pour the marinade over the beef. Before serving, snip over the chives.

Lamb cutlets with courgettes & mint

SERVES 2 / PREP TIME: 7 MINUTES / COOKING TIME: 15–20 MINUTES

Boiled vegetables are a no-no in this culinary age, but done the correct way they are delicate but delicious. Courgettes cooked by this method can be eaten either warm or cold. I prefer the former, drizzled with some dark green olive oil and topped with fresh goat's cheese, mint and a little sliced onion. Lamb cutlets are so tasty, all crispy and caramelised from the bone. Don't forget to pour over the juices from the pan.

4–6 lamb cutlets
4–6 medium courgettes, sliced
1 red onion, sliced into thin rings
1 heaped tablespoon crumbled soft goat's cheese
Maldon salt
freshly ground black pepper
extra virgin olive oil
a handful of fresh mint leaves, roughly chopped or left whole

Preheat the grill to high. Grill the lamb cutlets until well browned on both sides and cooked to taste.

Meanwhile, cook the courgettes in plenty of boiling salted water for 15–20 minutes or until tender. Drain well and transfer to a serving dish. Lay the onion rings on top and scatter over the goat's cheese and some salt and pepper. Drizzle over some olive oil and scatter with the mint. Serve with the chops.

three
vegetarian – for those who don't eat meat or fish

Summer vegetable soup

SERVES 2 / PREP TIME: 10 MINUTES / COOKING TIME: 15 MINUTES

I'm happy to have a cold soup in summer if it is given to me, but I really prefer warm soups. We need comforting in the summer too and this vegetable soup is both refreshing and wholesome. One of my favourite ways to enjoy soup is to take a large chunk of baguette smeared indulgently with unsalted butter and dunk it into the bowl.

extra virgin olive oil
1 garlic clove, crushed
1 leek, sliced
grated zest and juice of 1 lemon
500ml vegetable stock
1 tablespoon white short-grain rice
5 baby carrots, scrubbed
100g mangetout
1 courgette, finely chopped
80g shelled fresh or frozen peas
a small bunch of fresh chives, snipped
2 teaspoons freshly grated Parmesan

Drizzle a little olive oil into a saucepan and heat, then add the garlic, leek and lemon zest and cook for a couple of minutes until soft.

Add the stock and lemon juice and bring to the boil. Add the rice and stir until boiling again. Turn the heat down so the soup is simmering and cook for 10 minutes or until the rice is tender.

Add the carrots, mangetout, courgette and peas and cook for a few more minutes. Serve sprinkled with the chives and Parmesan.

Miso, ginger & udon noodle soup

SERVES 2 / PREP TIME: 10 MINUTES / COOKING TIME: 10 MINUTES

Miso soup can really hit the spot. It's warming and nourishing, and if accompanied by noodles and other goodies it can be a very satisfying meal. I do like slurping the broth out of the side of the bowl and fiddling with chopsticks to engineer the rest of the food into my mouth. If you have vegetables like broccoli or celery on hand, throw them all in. Enoki are the small white mushrooms with long stems and tiny heads, and udon are thick Japanese noodles. If you are a strict vegetarian, leave out the fish sauce and add a little more soy sauce to taste.

600ml spring water
2 tablespoons miso paste
1 tablespoon fish sauce
1 tablespoon sweet soy sauce
1 teaspoon grated fresh ginger
50g Asian greens, such as pak choy, shredded
150g fresh udon noodles
2 spring onions, sliced
40g enoki mushrooms
a few fresh coriander leaves

Put the water in a saucepan and add the miso, fish sauce and soy sauce. Set on a high heat and bring to the boil. Reduce the heat to a simmer.

Add the ginger, greens and noodles, and cook for a couple of minutes or until the noodles are tender. Add the spring onions and mushrooms to the soup and stir, then ladle into soup bowls. Place a couple of coriander leaves on top and serve immediately.

Avocado, roasted red onion & spinach salad

SERVES 2 / PREP TIME: 10 MINUTES / COOKING TIME: 20 MINUTES

This is a very straightforward salad of avocados and spinach, with the added attraction of hot onions, which cause the spinach to wilt a little. Roasting onions makes them sweet and tender, and they work perfectly with the lovely creamy quality of the avocados. If you cut open the avocados a bit early, squeeze over lemon juice so they don't turn brown.

1 red onion, cut into wedges
extra virgin olive oil
Maldon salt
100g baby spinach leaves
1 avocado, peeled, stoned and sliced

Dressing
2 teaspoons lemon juice
a few fresh flat-leaf parsley leaves, finely chopped
4 tablespoons extra virgin olive oil
1 teaspoon caster sugar
freshly ground black pepper

Preheat the oven to 200°C/gas 6. Place the onion wedges on a small baking tray, drizzle them with olive oil and sprinkle over a pinch of salt. Roast for about 20 minutes or until tender.

Combine the dressing ingredients in a jam jar, cover and give it a good shake. Season to taste with salt and pepper. Mix together the spinach and avocado in a salad bowl and add the hot onions and dressing. Toss together, then serve immediately. Crisp brown toast would be delicious with this.

Warm red lentil & baby spinach with a ginger dressing

SERVES 2 / PREP TIME: 10 MINUTES / COOKING TIME: 30 MINUTES

Lentils are very nutritious – high in protein, starchy carbohydrate and fibre but very low in fat. Unlike other pulses they don't need to be soaked before cooking, so are really convenient. For this recipe I've cooked them like a risotto.

extra virgin olive oil
2 garlic cloves, crushed
200g split red lentils
600ml vegetable stock
Maldon salt
freshly ground black pepper
150g baby spinach leaves

Dressing
grated zest and juice of 1/2 lemon
4 tablespoons extra virgin olive oil
1 teaspoon grated fresh ginger
a pinch of paprika
1 teaspoon caster sugar

Coat the bottom of a saucepan with olive oil and gently sauté the garlic until soft. Add the lentils and let them cook for a couple of minutes, then turn them in the olive oil. Gradually add the stock, simmering until all the liquid has been absorbed. Cooking time will be about 25 minutes. Add a little more liquid if the lentils are not tender. Season to taste with salt and pepper.

In a salad bowl, combine the lemon zest and juice and the olive oil. Whisk in the ginger, paprika, sugar and a pinch of salt. Toss the spinach in the dressing, then spoon over the warm lentils. Season to taste and eat immediately.

Another idea: Bulghur wheat salad with garden herbs, kumquats & almonds

Soak 40g of bulghur wheat in cold water for 10 minutes. Drain and squeeze to remove any excess water. Place the wheat in a serving bowl. Season with salt and pepper, then drizzle generously with extra virgin olive oil. Mix in the following ingredients, all finely chopped: a small handful of fresh flat-leaf parsley leaves, a small handful of fresh basil leaves, a small handful of fresh coriander leaves, a small handful of fresh mint leaves, 2 teaspoons of almonds, 4–6 kumquats and 2 spring onions. Taste for seasoning, then serve.

Asparagus, pecorino & courgette salad with a mint & lemon dressing

SERVES 2 / PREP TIME: 10 MINUTES / COOKING TIME: 10 MINUTES

To cook asparagus successfully, you don't need a large steamer. Simply lay the spears in one layer in a wide pan, cover with water and boil gently. For this salad I like to cook courgettes the Italian way – cut in long slices, brushed with olive oil and garlic, and grilled. To munch alongside, toast some delicious rustic or country bread, wipe it with a garlic clove and drizzle over a little of your best extra virgin olive oil (the darker green the better).

500g asparagus
2 medium-to-large courgettes
2 garlic cloves, crushed
extra virgin olive oil
5 baby spring onions, cut lengthways into quarters
a small handful of rocket
a small chunk of pecorino cheese

Dressing
4 tablespoons extra virgin olive oil
juice of 1/2 lemon
1 garlic clove, crushed
1 teaspoon caster sugar
a few sprigs of fresh mint, leaves only, finely chopped
Maldon salt
freshly ground black pepper

For the dressing, combine the ingredients in a jam jar. Cover and give it a good shake. Season to taste with salt and pepper.

Preheat the grill to high. Trim off the woody ends of the asparagus stalks. Cook the asparagus either in a tall steamer or a wide pan (salt the water if poaching) until it is soft but still has that essential crunch. Meanwhile, cut the courgettes into long strips, neither too thin nor too thick. Spread some crushed garlic over the slices, then brush them with olive oil. Grill until they are a little charred and just tender.

Drain the asparagus and place it in a bowl with the courgettes, spring onions and rocket. Using a vegetable peeler, slice a few pecorino shavings on top. Pour over the dressing, toss and eat while still warm.

Green couscous with a beetroot salsa

SERVES 2 / PREP TIME: 15 MINUTES / COOKING TIME: 7 MINUTES (PLUS ROASTING THE BEETROOTS)

Couscous is a delicious alternative to rice and is happy with most other foods. I love to work with colours and in themes – hence this green couscous with a red salsa. If you can, cook your own beetroots. My favourite way is to roast them in their skins, just until they are al dente (see page 136), then to peel and chop them. If you are in a hurry you can buy them ready cooked, but you won't be able to enjoy the real flavour and texture that you get from home-cooked beetroots.

Couscous

200g couscous
a handful of green beans
3 spring onions, finely chopped
a few fresh mint leaves, finely chopped
2 teaspoons chopped fresh chives
1/4 cucumber, peeled and chopped
juice of 1/2 lemon
extra virgin olive oil

Beetroot salsa

2 teaspoons extra virgin olive oil
1 teaspoon lemon juice
1/2 teaspoon soft brown sugar
2 small cooked beetroots, peeled and finely chopped
1/2 red apple, cored and diced
a few slices of red onion, finely chopped
a small handful of walnuts, chopped
Maldon salt
freshly ground black pepper

First make the salsa. In a small bowl, mix together the olive oil, lemon juice and sugar, then add the remaining salsa ingredients. Mix well and season with salt and pepper. Set aside.

Steam the couscous as per the packet instructions. Meanwhile, steam the green beans until just tender but still crisp.

Spoon the couscous into a warm serving dish. Stir in the green beans, spring onions, mint, chives, cucumber, lemon juice and olive oil. Season well. Serve immediately with the salsa and some Moroccan flat bread.

Polenta with Parmesan & grilled figs

SERVES 1–2 / PREP TIME: 10 MINUTES / COOKING TIME: 30 MINUTES

Polenta is both a meal ground from corn and the name of the dish that is made from it – one of the oldest dishes in Italian cooking. If you have any polenta left over, pour it into a tray and let it set, then slice, brush it lightly with extra virgin olive oil and grill on both sides. Add a topping such as sautéed mushrooms or tomatoes and mozzarella with herbs, and enjoy.

about 200ml water
150g polenta
Maldon salt
15g unsalted butter
2 tablespoons freshly grated Parmesan, plus shavings
2–4 figs
extra virgin olive oil
a few radicchio leaves
balsamic vinegar
freshly ground black pepper

Put the water in a saucepan and bring to the boil. Pour in the polenta, stirring constantly with a wooden spoon so that it doesn't become lumpy, and add a pinch of salt. Reduce the heat and simmer, regularly scraping the polenta down from the sides of the pan, for about 30 minutes. Stir in the butter and grated Parmesan and cook for a few more minutes.

While the polenta is cooking, preheat the grill to high. Cut the figs crossways into slices and grill for a couple of minutes or until they are beginning to crisp.

Pour the polenta on to a warm plate and lay the figs on top. Scatter over the Parmesan shavings and add a drizzle of olive oil. Dress the radicchio leaves with olive oil and balsamic vinegar, season to taste with salt and pepper and serve alongside the polenta.

Field mushrooms with thyme on fried bread

SERVES 1–2 / PREP TIME: 5 MINUTES / COOKING TIME: 12 MINUTES

This is a recipe for autumn when mushrooms are at their best. I favour the large brown field mushrooms, but I like to mix them with other types of mushrooms. Serving the mushrooms on fried bread adds a filling richness to this dish. I also think a pint of chilled stout enhances them.

30g unsalted butter
1 garlic clove, crushed
250g mixed mushrooms, roughly chopped
2 sprigs of fresh thyme, leaves only
Maldon salt
freshly ground black pepper
extra virgin olive oil
1–2 slices of white farmhouse bread, crusts removed

Melt the butter in a frying pan and, when sizzling, add the garlic. Cook until soft, then add the mushrooms and two-thirds of the thyme leaves. Season well with salt and pepper. Sauté until the mushrooms are tender. Remove from the pan and keep hot.

Liberally coat the bottom of the frying pan with olive oil. When it is hot, fry the bread on a high heat until crisp and golden on both sides. Drain the fried bread on kitchen paper to absorb any excess oil, then place the slices on one or two serving plates. Spoon over the mushrooms, add a little more salt and pepper, and garnish with the remaining thyme leaves. Serve immediately.

Bruschetta with roast tomatoes, onions & basil

SERVES 2 / PREP TIME: 10 MINUTES / COOKING TIME: 20 MINUTES

When roasted, tomatoes are much sweeter and have a richer texture than when they are raw. Roasting is also a good way of using overripe tomatoes. This bruschetta combines tomatoes and basil, which is one of the soulmate pairings of the kitchen. I like copious amounts of garlic rubbed on the toasted bread before it soaks up the peppery Tuscan extra virgin olive oil.

4 fresh plum tomatoes, preferably Italian
1 small red onion, sliced
Maldon salt
Tuscan extra virgin olive oil
4 slices of sourdough bread
1 garlic clove, peeled
a handful of fresh basil leaves
freshly ground black pepper

Preheat the oven to 200°C/gas 6. Place the tomatoes and onions in a roasting dish, sprinkle over a little salt and add a drizzle of olive oil. Place in the oven and roast for 20 minutes.

Toast the bread, then rub with the garlic clove and drizzle over some olive oil. Place a couple of onion rings on each slice of toast, then gently squash a tomato on top and finish with a basil leaf. Season with salt and pepper and eat immediately, with a large napkin on hand.

Rosemary, Parmesan & tomato pizza

SERVES 2 / PREP TIME: 25 MINUTES PLUS 2–3 HOURS RISING

COOKING TIME: 15 MINUTES

I haven't mastered making round pizza bases and spinning them in the air, so I can only give you instructions on how to make a rectangular or square pizza. Be adventurous in deciding what to put on the top. This is a pizza topping I like, but you could go for caramelised onions and olives, mozzarella, rocket and chilli, or whatever you fancy.

Crust

200g plain flour, sifted
1/2 teaspoon Maldon salt
1/2 sachet easy-blend dried yeast, about 7g
about 115ml warm water
1 tablespoon extra virgin olive oil

Topping

2 small tomatoes, preferably 1 red and 1 yellow, sliced
5 black olives, pitted and halved
40g Parmesan, thinly sliced
1 1/2 tablespoons chopped fresh rosemary
Maldon salt
extra virgin olive oil

To make the pizza crust, put the flour, salt and yeast into a large mixing bowl. Make a well in the centre and add the warm water and olive oil. Mix all the ingredients with a wooden spoon, then knead the dough on a floured surface with floury hands for about 10 minutes or until elastic and smooth. Oil the bowl with a little olive oil. Put the dough in the bowl and turn so that it is coated with oil. Cover with a clean cloth and leave to rise in a warm place for 2–3 hours (I sometimes leave it longer). If you feel at any time that you would like to give the dough a punch or two, go for it.

Preheat the oven to 200°C/gas 6. By now the dough will have doubled in size and have a spongy texture. Knead it for a minute or two, then flatten the ball with a rolling pin. Divide in half and roll out into two rectangles as thin as possible. Place the pizza bases on one or two oiled baking trays.

Divide the tomato slices and olives evenly between the bases. Scatter the Parmesan slices over the tomatoes, then sprinkle with the rosemary and a light dusting of salt. Finish with a little extra drizzle of olive oil. Bake the pizzas on the top shelf of the oven until the crust is golden and crisp. Serve immediately.

Crisp baby tarts with goat's cheese, red onions & oregano

SERVES 2 / PREP TIME: 10 MINUTES / COOKING TIME: 15–20 MINUTES

When I'm in a restaurant, I order any dish with goat's cheese. And I hunt down goat's cheeses wherever I am, particularly in markets in France. Cooked goat's cheese and pastry have a pleasing affinity, and these are particularly pretty little tarts, with the red of the onions and the green leaves of the oregano. Serve with a few Oak Leaf lettuce leaves tossed in extra virgin olive oil and balsamic vinegar.

plain flour
200g puff pastry, thawed if frozen
125g firm goat's cheese
1 small red onion, thinly sliced
4 sprigs of fresh oregano
Maldon sea salt
4 teaspoons milk
freshly ground black pepper

Preheat the oven to 200°C/gas 6 and oil a baking tray with a little oil. Sprinkle some flour on a work surface and unroll or unfold the pastry. Cut out two square shapes that are 10–15cm on each side and put them on the baking tray.

Break or cut the goat's cheese into small cubes and place in the centre of the pastry squares. (You can make the pile quite high, as the pastry will rise up around it.) Scatter over the onion and lay one sprig of oregano on top of each pile. Season with salt. Brush the edges of the pastry squares with milk, then bake for 15–20 minutes or until the pastry is all puffed up, crispy and golden.

Replace the oregano with fresh sprigs and season with pepper, then serve.

Another idea: Caramelised onion & pimentón parcels with Manchego cheese

Preheat the oven to 180°C/gas 4. Heat 4 teaspoons of extra virgin olive oil in a saucepan and add 4 small red onions, sliced, 1 teaspoon of soft brown sugar and 3/4 teaspoon of pimentón. Cook until the onions are tender.

On a floured board roll out 350g puff pastry and cut into four squares. Divide 100g grated Manchego cheese among the squares, piling it in the middle. Spoon the onions over the cheese and season with salt and pepper. Take the four corners of each pastry square and pull them into the middle. Glaze the pastry with milk. Transfer to a baking tray oiled with a little oil and bake for 25 minutes or until golden and puffed. Serve hot.

Leek & potato vinaigrette with crumbled egg & chives

SERVES 1–2 / PREP TIME: 15 MINUTES / COOKING TIME: ABOUT 20 MINUTES

This is a recipe I remember well from my childhood, as my grandmothers often used to make it. I like to crumble the egg with a fork, but if you have one of those natty little egg slicers crying out to be used, retrieve it from the drawer and slice away – whatever is more aesthetically pleasing to you. For a change you could use quail's eggs, which look rather cute sliced. I'm not sure that egg slicers cater for quail's eggs, so you'll probably just have to use a knife.

400g waxy potatoes such as Pink Fir Apple
6 thin young leeks, whole
1 large egg, hard-boiled and crumbled or sliced
a small handful of fresh chives, snipped
4 pitted black Provençal olives, finely chopped

Dressing
1 garlic clove, crushed with a pinch of salt
1 teaspoon Dijon mustard
2 tablespoons white wine vinegar
3 tablespoons mild olive oil
a pinch of Maldon salt

Cook the potatoes in boiling salted water until just tender; drain. When cool enough to handle, peel them. While the potatoes are cooking, steam the leeks until just cooked. You don't want them to be soggy or to lose too much colour.

In a small bowl or jam jar, mix together all of the dressing ingredients until amalgamated. Arrange the warm leeks and potatoes in a salad bowl or serving dish and pour over the dressing. Scatter over the egg, chives and olives, and serve immediately.

Baked potato with hot feta, chilli, oregano & lamb's lettuce salad

SERVES 2 / PREP TIME: 10 MINUTES / COOKING TIME: ABOUT 40 MINUTES

Sometimes a good baked potato for supper fits the bill perfectly, especially when it is accessorised with the freshest of ingredients. There's a bit of a rut when it comes to fillings for baked potatoes – usually grated cheese and a slab of butter, perhaps with a dollop of baked beans. That can be quite good, but if you're feeling a little more adventurous then try this. It couldn't be an easier meal.

2 small baking potatoes
1 small packet of feta cheese
extra virgin olive oil
1/2 small red chilli, deseeded and finely chopped
a few sprigs of fresh oregano
2 handfuls of lamb's lettuce
Maldon salt

Preheat the oven to 190°C/gas 5. Stab the potatoes here and there with a fork, then place them in the oven and bake until soft. (Make sure the potatoes aren't touching, as this will slow down the cooking.)

Break the feta into pieces, put it in a saucepan with a drizzle of olive oil and the chilli, and set on a moderate heat. When the feta is becoming hot and the oil is slightly sizzling, remove from the heat.

Remove the potatoes from the oven and slam them down on a wooden board. This makes them fluffy inside. Cut them in half, put them on plates and pour over the feta mixture. Squeeze the oregano in the palm of your hand to release the oils, then break off the leaves and sprinkle them over the potato. Add a handfull of lamb's lettuce to each plate, drizzle some olive oil over it and add a sprinkle of salt. Serve immediately.

Baked fennel with Parmesan & ciabatta breadcrumbs

SERVES 2 / PREP TIME: 15 MINUTES / COOKING TIME: 20 MINUTES

For years, whenever I was buying my vegetables I'd pause momentarily in front of a shelf of fennel, contemplate the strange pleated ivory bulb with green shadows and protruding stalks with their feathery leaves, and be really quite perplexed as to how to tackle it. I always thought, leave it to the restaurants or someone else. Today, though, fennel is a regular part of my shopping. It is delicious slipped into salads and, with its distinct anise flavour, it is a little bit of an aristocrat in the vegetable world. With just a little accessorising it makes a sophisticated and subtle dish. As there is a vague Italian theme here, I suggest you use an Italian wine such as a Pinot Grigio in the dish, and drink the rest.

2–3 fennel bulbs
15g dry ciabatta breadcrumbs
40g Parmesan, finely grated
1/2 tablespoon extra virgin olive oil
Maldon sea salt
50ml dry white wine

Preheat the oven to 150°C/gas 2. Slice off the base of the fennel bulbs and trim the stalks, keeping the feathery parts for the garnish. Cut the bulbs lengthways in half and cut out the core. Place the fennel halves cut side up in an ovenproof dish. In a bowl, mix together the breadcrumbs, Parmesan, olive oil and salt to taste. Sprinkle the mixture over the fennel, then splash over the white wine. Bake for about 20 minutes or until the fennel is tender. Scatter over the feathery bits and serve immediately.

Pecorino & Parmesan souffle

SERVES 2 / PREP TIME: 15 MINUTES / COOKING TIME: 25 MINUTES

Soufflés are what well-brought-up young ladies of my mother's generation wanted to master – the Fifties' housewife in a neat pinny with a proper hairdo, presenting a fluffy, perfectly risen soufflé to her discerning husband. I think the soufflé died out with the rise of feminism. But they are deeply rewarding to make and not as difficult as you might think. I like the sense of urgency in getting this bouffant dish from the oven to the table without it deflating, then enjoying the beauty of its formation and the liquidy, spongy interior. The difference between a Fifties' housewife and a woman today is that he who does not do the cooking gets to clean up, and this is not a low-maintenance dish.

30g unsalted butter, plus extra for greasing
4 medium eggs, separated, plus 1 egg white
40g plain flour
250ml milk, warmed
40g Parmesan, freshly grated
40g pecorino cheese, freshly grated
1 tablespoon finely chopped fresh flat-leaf parsley
Maldon salt
freshly ground black pepper

Preheat the oven to 200°C/gas 6. Grease a 750ml soufflé dish with unsalted butter; put to one side. Whisk the egg yolks in a small bowl. In another, larger bowl whisk the egg whites until soft peaks have formed. Melt the butter in a saucepan, stir in the flour and then slowly add the warm milk. Cook, stirring, for a few minutes until the mixture thickens. Remove from the heat and whisk in the egg yolks until smooth and creamy. Add the cheeses, stirring them in slowly, then add the parsley and season with a pinch of salt and pepper to taste. Very carefully fold in about one-quarter of the egg whites, always making an upward motion. Then add the rest of the egg whites, folding in as gently as possible – the mixture should look cloudy on top.

Gently pour the mixture into the soufflé dish and pop it into the oven. Turn down the temperature after 5 minutes to 190°C/gas 5 and bake for a further 20 minutes or until the soufflé looks golden, puffy and delicious. Do not open the oven door during baking or the soufflé will sink.

Spaghetti with spring onions, Gorgonzola & chives

SERVES 2 / PREP TIME: 12 MINUTES / COOKING TIME: 15 MINUTES

This dish is on the rich side as it is made with a creamy cheese, some cream and wine, so you'll probably find you won't want a big portion. It's also really pretty, all creamy and green with scattered snipped chives. Gorgonzola, a blue-veined Italian cheese, can vary in pungency depending on the producer, so you might want to taste it before adding it to the sauce and use more or less cheese as required. Also, add some of the pasta cooking water to thin the sauce. I think a glass of Pino Nero works wonders with this dish.

150g spaghetti
2 knobs of unsalted butter
8 spring onions, sliced
125g Gorgonzola cheese
a pinch of vegetable bouillon powder
2 tablespoons single cream
a generous splash of white wine
Maldon salt
freshly ground black pepper
a bunch of fresh chives

Cook the spaghetti in a large pan of boiling salted water as per the packet instructions, until al dente. Meanwhile, melt a knob of butter in a frying pan and gently sauté the spring onions until soft. Stir in the Gorgonzola and let it melt, then sprinkle over the bouillon powder and stir in the cream. Let it simmer gently for a moment or two, then add the wine and 3 tablespoons of the cooking water from the spaghetti. Simmer to reduce slightly.

Drain the spaghetti and return to the pan. Taste the sauce and season with salt and pepper, adding more cheese if required, then pour the sauce over the pasta in the pan. Add the other knob of butter. Set over a moderate heat and mix the pasta and sauce really well, snipping over the chives as you do and mixing them in well. Check the seasoning and serve pronto.

Courgette, capers, lemon zest & parsley linguini

SERVES 2 / PREP TIME: 10 MINUTES / COOKING TIME: 15 MINUTES

Capers are the flower bud of a Mediterranean shrub. They can only be eaten once they have been pickled, which gives them their characteristic sharp, slightly bitter flavour. They are delicious used sparingly and give an unexpected piquancy to this pasta dish. When I make it I go somewhat overboard with the Parmesan, so that every strand of linguini is coated thickly. If you don't have any capers in the cupboard, the recipe will still work. If you don't have linguini go for spaghetti.

175g linguini
extra virgin olive oil
1 shallot, finely chopped
1 large garlic clove, crushed
3 courgettes, grated
Maldon salt
freshly ground black pepper
a knob of unsalted butter
grated zest of 1 small lemon
2 teaspoons small capers, rinsed and drained
a handful of fresh flat-leaf parsley leaves
at least 70g Parmesan, freshly grated

Add the linguini to a big pan of boiling salted water and cook as per the packet instructions, until al dente.

Meanwhile, coat the bottom of a frying pan with olive oil. When it is hot, add the shallot and garlic and cook until soft. Add the courgettes and cook over a low to moderate heat for 7–10 minutes or until soft but still retaining a little bite. Add more olive oil if you feel the courgettes are too dry, as they absorb a lot of oil. Season well with salt and pepper.

Drain the pasta. Put the butter in the pasta pan and place the pasta on top. Add the lemon zest, capers and most of the parsley to the courgettes and pour this over the pasta. Combine well, mixing in the Parmesan. Cook over a moderate heat for a couple of minutes so that all the ingredients can blend. Check the seasoning, then divide between two hot plates. Place a couple of parsley leaves on the top of each serving and grate over some more Parmesan.

four
indulge – richer comfort food

Chicken & corn chowder

SERVES 2 / PREP TIME: 10 MINUTES / COOKING TIME: 20-30 MINUTES

So often the carcass of Sunday's roast chicken sits expectantly in the fridge, slowly drying out, and then gets binned by Wednesday. This is a shame, because it could have been used in this delicious chowder for supper on Monday night. To put the chicken carcass to work, first take off as much of the meat as you can – don't forget the oysters, which are the two fleshy pillows on either side underneath. Use the bones to make a great stock for future use in gravies, casseroles or soups, If you don't have any leftover chicken, you'll need to buy two breasts for this chowder; drizzle over some olive oil and grill them until cooked.

extra virgin olive oil
4 bacon rashers
1 small onion, finely chopped
3 garlic cloves, finely chopped
leftover cooked chicken equal to 2 chicken breasts, cut into small chunks
2 corn on the cob, kernels sliced off
1 litre chicken stock
6–8 small new potatoes
4 spring onions, whole
142ml double cream
Maldon salt
freshly ground black pepper
a handful of fresh flat-leaf parsley leaves, roughly chopped

Preheat the oven to 170°C/gas 3. Swirl some olive oil over the bottom of a flameproof earthenware or enamel casserole. When hot, cook the bacon until brown. Throw in the onion and garlic and cook until soft, then add the chicken and corn kernels and stir-fry for a few minutes. Cover with the stock, put the lid on the casserole and transfer to the oven. Cook for 15 minutes.

Stir in the potatoes. Re-cover the casserole, return to the oven and cook for 10 minutes. Add the spring onions and cook, covered, for a further 5 minutes. Remove from the oven and stir in the cream. Season well with salt and pepper and scatter over the parsley leaves. Serve in soup bowls with a fresh baguette.

Creamy leek & haddock soup

SERVES 2 / PREP TIME: 15 MINUTES / COOKING TIME: 20 MINUTES

This soup truly is a meal in itself. It's warm and creamy with the comfort of potatoes and the smoky deliciousness of haddock tinged with the fresh savouriness of parsley. Serve with really fresh wholegrain bread spread with lashings of unsalted butter.

4 small potatoes, peeled
a knob of unsalted butter
1 tablespoon extra virgin olive oil
1 red onion, roughly chopped
2 large leeks, sliced into discs
600ml fish stock
300g undyed smoked haddock, skinned and cut into medium to small chunks
125ml double cream
Maldon salt
freshly ground black pepper
a small bunch of fresh flat-leaf parsley, leaves only

Cook the potatoes in plenty of boiling salted water until tender. Drain well and cut into small chunks. Set aside. Heat the butter and olive oil in a large saucepan, add the onion and leeks and sauté gently until soft. Add the stock and bring it to simmering point. Add the potatoes and haddock and simmer for about 5 minutes. Stir in the cream, then season to taste with salt and pepper. Scatter over the parsley and serve immediately.

Macaroni with four cheeses

SERVES 2 / PREP TIME: 10 MINUTES / COOKING TIME: 20 MINUTES

Making macaroni cheese with four different cheeses gives a much richer, more sophisticated dish. You'll find it quite filling, so a fresh green salad with mustard dressing is a good contrast. If you can't find all the cheeses replace one of them with Parmesan or Emmental.

135g macaroni
25g unsalted butter
3/4 teaspoon plain flour
300ml milk
15g mozzarella, grated
15g Gruyère cheese, grated
15g fontina cheese, grated
15g Provolone cheese, grated
15g Parmesan, freshly grated
Maldon salt
freshly ground black pepper
a few fresh flat-leaf parsley leaves

Preheat the grill to high. Cook the macaroni in plenty of boiling salted water as per the packet instructions, until al dente.

Meanwhile, melt the butter in a saucepan and stir in the flour. Slowly add the milk, stirring constantly with a wooden spoon, and cook, stirring, until the sauce thickens. Stir in all of the cheeses except for the Parmesan and cook gently for a few minutes so that all the cheeses melt together. Season the sauce well with salt and pepper.

Drain the macaroni thoroughly and place it in an ovenproof dish. Pour over the cheese sauce, then sprinkle the grated Parmesan evenly over the top. Place the dish under the grill for a couple of minutes, until the cheese begins to bubble and brown. Sprinkle with parsley and serve.

Smoked cod & salmon baked in cream

SERVES 2 / PREP TIME: 10 MINUTES / COOKING TIME: 20 MINUTES

This is a really easy, no-fuss fish dinner. The smokiness of the fish permeates through the cream, the tomatoes add sweetness, and the herbs provide flavour accent and freshness. Seek out some red rice from the Camargue or some wild rice to serve alongside.

150g undyed smoked cod fillet, cut into 5cm cubes
150g naturally lightly smoked salmon fillet, cut into 5cm cubes
a bunch of fresh chives
275ml double cream
2 beef tomatoes, sliced
Maldon salt
freshly ground black pepper
1 heaped teaspoon sugar
a small bunch of fresh flat-leaf parsley, finely chopped
a small bunch of fresh basil, leaves only, torn

Preheat the oven to 190°C/gas 5. Place the smoked cod and salmon in an ovenproof dish. Snip over a generous sprinkling of chives. Pour over the cream and cover with the sliced tomatoes. Season them with salt and pepper and sprinkle with the sugar.

Bake for about 20 minutes or until it is bubbling at the sides. Remove from the oven and scatter over the fresh parsley and basil, then serve.

Cod, prawn & parsley pie

SERVES 4–6 / PREP TIME: 20 MINUTES / COOKING TIME: 30 MINUTES

A fish pie can really hit the spot – all that creamy mashed potato mixed with flaking cod and pink prawns in a velvety-smooth sauce. I think peas go better with fish pie than any other vegetable, and frozen ones are so good. Try to find petis pois, as they are sweeter than regular peas. Cook them gently in butter with a little chopped mint and some salt and pepper.

275ml fish stock
a glass of dry white wine
3 bay leaves
1 teaspoon green peppercorns
1kg fresh cod fillet
50g unsalted butter
50g plain flour
1 tablespoon crème fraîche
a bunch of fresh flat-leaf parsley, leaves only, finely chopped
5 handfuls of cooked prawns, peeled

Topping
900g floury potatoes, such as Desiree
unsalted butter
milk
Maldon salt
freshly ground black pepper

Preheat the oven to 200°C/gas 6. Cook the potatoes in plenty of boiling salted water until soft when pricked with a fork. Drain well and return to the pan. Mash with butter (as much as you want) until there are no lumps, then slowly add enough milk to make the mash creamy. Season to taste with salt and pepper.

While the potatoes are cooking, heat the stock and wine with the bay leaves and peppercorns in a saucepan. Cut the fish into pieces to fit in the pan and poach in the liquid for about 5 minutes. It should be undercooked. Remove the fish to a plate and allow to cool. Strain the liquid and reserve.

Melt the butter in another saucepan and stir in the flour, then slowly stir in the reserved liquid. Simmer until thickened. Turn the heat to low and stir in the crème fraîche and parsley. Cook gently for a few minutes, then season well with salt and pepper.

Remove the skin from the fish and divide it into large chunks. Place evenly in a pie dish and scatter over the prawns. Pour over the sauce. Gently spoon the mashed potatoes on top, without pressing it down too much. Bake for 45–50 minutes or until the top is lightly browned and crisp and you can see the sauce bubbling up. Serve hot.

Fusilli with pancetta, chestnuts & sage

SERVES 2 / PREP TIME: 15 MINUTES / COOKING TIME: 20 MINUTES

Chestnuts are a popular ingredient during the winter months. They have a lovely rich, creamy quality. If you have the time buy them fresh, and boil and peel them yourself. Otherwise you can use ready cooked chestnuts in jars. This is a rich dish. A winter salad of radicchio and basil would work well on the side with a full-bodied white Burgundy to wash it down.

250g fusilli
5 slices of pancetta
2 shallots, finely chopped
1 garlic clove, crushed
a small bunch of fresh sage, leaves only
1 teaspoon Vin Santo
200ml double cream
75g Parmesan, freshly grated
8 chestnuts, cooked and peeled
Maldon salt
freshly ground black pepper

Cook the pasta in a big pan of boiling salted water as per packet instructions, until al dente.

Meanwhile, fry the pancetta in a large frying pan until crisp. Remove with tongs, shaking off any excess oil, and chop roughly. Add the shallots and garlic to the fat in the pan and sauté until soft. (Add some extra virgin olive oil if needed.) Throw in most of the sage leaves, then stir in the Vin Santo, cream and 2 teaspoons of the Parmesan. Let the sauce bubble away gently for a few minutes, then mix in the chestnuts and pancetta. Season to taste with salt and pepper.

Drain the pasta and add it to the sauce in the frying pan. Cook on a high heat for a couple of minutes, mixing well. Serve sprinkled with the remaining Parmesan and sage leaves.

Gnocchi with Jerusalem artichokes, bacon & onions

SERVES 2 / PREP TIME: 10 MINUTES / COOKING TIME: 20 MINUTES

The Jerusalem artichoke does not come from Jerusalem and has nothing to do with the globe artichoke. Surprisingly, it's actually related to the sunflower. It has a slightly sweet taste that works beautifully with the saltiness of bacon. Fresh sage rounds off all the flavours in this dish most satisfactorily.

extra virgin olive oil
1 large red onion, sliced into rings
1 garlic clove, crushed
6 streaky bacon rashers, chopped into short strips
6 Jerusalem artichokes, peeled and thinly sliced into discs
4 fresh sage leaves, finely chopped, plus extra whole leaves to garnish
Maldon salt
freshly ground black pepper
4 teaspoons double cream
60g Parmesan, freshly grated
600g fresh gnocchi

Drizzle some olive oil in a frying pan and, when hot, sauté the onion and garlic for a few minutes. Add the bacon and cook for a few more minutes, then add the artichokes and chopped sage. Season to taste with salt and pepper. Cook gently for 15 minutes or until the artichokes are just tender. Turn down the heat to very low and stir in the cream and two-thirds of the Parmesan. Keep the sauce hot.

Add the gnocchi to a saucepan of boiling salted water. When they bob up to the top they are ready. Drain well, then throw the gnocchi into the frying pan with the sauce and stir it all together. Turn up the heat and cook for a minute or so. Serve topped with the last of the Parmesan and two whole sage leaves to garnish.

Parmesan & prosciutto baked eggs

SERVES 2 / PREP TIME: 10 MINUTES / COOKING TIME: 25 MINUTES

This is an Italian take on an old favourite and it's a delightful savoury. If you haven't got Parmesan and prosciutto, but there's Cheddar cheese and bacon in your fridge, these will work just as well, as long as you fry or grill the bacon first. Loads of thin, buttery white toast should be on hand to serve with the eggs.

25g unsalted butter
4 slices of prosciutto, finely chopped
4 teaspoons finely chopped fresh flat-leaf parsley
4 medium eggs
Maldon salt
freshly ground black pepper
2 tablespoons freshly grated Parmesan

Preheat the oven to 180°C/gas 4. Liberally grease two large ramekins with butter, then set them in a roasting tin half filled with water. Divide the prosciutto and most of the parsley among the ramekins. Break two eggs into each ramekin, season well with salt and pepper and sprinkle the Parmesan over the top. Put the roasting tin into the oven and bake for 25 minutes or until the eggs are set. Sprinkle with the remaining parsley and serve hot.

Another idea: Celeriac gratin with Parmesan, ham & cream

Preheat the oven to 200°C/gas 6. Grease the bottom of an ovenproof dish with plenty of butter. Peel and slice 2 medium to large potatoes and 1 medium celeriac. Shred 4 slices of honey roast ham. Make a layer of potatoes on the bottom of the dish, then add a layer of ham, then celeriac. Season well with salt and pepper. Repeat the layering until the dish is full, then dot with butter and pour over 240ml double cream. Bake for 30 minutes. Sprinkle with 75g Parmesan, freshly grated, and bake for a further 15 minutes or until golden and bubbling. Before serving sprinkle with a small handful of finely chopped fresh flat-leaf parsley.

Stuffed peppers with salami, thyme & onions

SERVES 2 / PREP TIME: 10 MINUTES / COOKING TIME: 30 MINUTES

This is a fun little dish with a slightly quirky quality to it – the peppers sit all formally, storing a surprise inside. For the stuffing you can use combinations of so many different ingredients – experiment with anything you like and that you feel will work. I've gone for three different types of Italian salami. Brianza, which is exclusively made from pork bred in the Lombardy, Piedmont and Romagna regions, is dry cured and fully matured. Napoli piccante is seasoned with paprika, white wine and red chilli, while Milano is a very traditional Italian salami that is seasoned with pepper and garlic. I cook the salami with some breadcrumbs and thyme, which work wonders with the peppers.

4 medium to large red peppers
extra virgin olive oil
2 small red onions, finely chopped
2 garlic cloves, finely chopped
6 slices of Milano salami, chopped
6 slices of Napoli piccante, chopped
6 slices of Brianza salami, chopped
2 tablespoons breadcrumbs
2 sprigs of fresh thyme, leaves only

Preheat the oven to 180°C/gas 4. Just before you chop the salami and onions, cut the tops off the peppers and scrape out the membranes and seeds. If the peppers won't stand upright, shave a little off the bases to make them stable. Put the peppers, standing upright, plus the tops in a roasting dish in the oven.

Prepare all the other ingredients. Swirl some olive oil over the bottom of a frying pan and heat it, then add the onions, garlic, salami, breadcrumbs and thyme. Cook for about 5 minutes or until the onions are soft.

Remove the peppers from the oven and carefully fill them with the salami mixture, trying not to add too much of the oil. Cover them with their tops, then put them back into the oven and cook for a further 15–20 minutes or until they look soft. Transfer the stuffed peppers to hot plates and serve with a green salad and/or some fried potatoes.

Cumberland sausage with a roasted apple, sage & onion relish

SERVES 2 / PREP TIME: 10 MINUTES / COOKING TIME: 20 MINUTES

There are so many new varieties of sausages, but I think the traditional is still the best. Cumberland sausage is made from a coarse cut of pork and it is somewhat spicier than most. It is traditionally sold in a coil rather than twisted into links. Butchers still sell it like this, but if you can't source it just go for the normal links.

2 Braeburn apples, cut into wedges and cored
1 red onion, cut into wedges
1 tablespoon extra virgin olive oil
Maldon salt
freshly ground black pepper
3 tablespoons apple cider
75g soft brown sugar
3 tablespoons water
4 fresh sage leaves
1 coil of Cumberland sausage

Preheat the oven to 200°C/gas 6. Place the apples and onion in a roasting tin and toss with olive oil, salt and pepper. Roast for about 20 minutes or until they are caramelised.

Meanwhile, combine the cider vinegar, brown sugar, water and sage leaves in a saucepan. Heat, stirring, until the sugar dissolves, then bring to simmering point and cook for 7–10 minutes or until the liquid becomes syrupy. Allow to cool a bit, then mix with the apple and onion mixture. Keep warm.

Coil the sausage in a large frying pan and drizzle with a tiny amount of olive oil, just so that it doesn't stick to the pan. Prick the sausage randomly. Cook on a moderate heat until golden brown on both sides and gooey. Chop into chunks or links and serve with the relish and mashed potato.

Another idea: Roast sausages with honey, rosemary & horseradish

Preheat the oven to 170°C/gas 3. Place 6 sausages, 6 peeled shallots and 2 sprigs of rosemary in a roasting tin. Drizzle with olive oil and 2 heaped teaspoons of runny honey. Put in the oven and roast for 35–40 minutes or until the sausages are crispy and the shallots caramelised. Remove the sausages and rosemary. Add 2 heaped teaspoons of horseradish cream to the juices in the tin and mix well. Season with salt. Roll the sausages in the sticky sauce. Eat immediately.

Roast Toulouse sausages with pan-fried fennel, leeks & thyme

SERVES 2 / PREP TIME: 7 MINUTES / COOKING TIME: 20 MINUTES

Toulouse sausages are a combination of pork, veal and herbs, so they are a little more interesting than your average pork sausage. I like to cook them in the oven. It does take longer than grilling or frying, but the outside becomes sticky and gooey and the inside meat seems to cook better. Also, you don't have to deal with all that fat spluttering at you. Fennel quickly fried in oil with leeks and thyme gives good back-up to the sausages and takes only a few minutes to throw together. A light Bordeaux will wash it all down swimmingly.

2–4 Toulouse sausages
extra virgin olive oil
1 fennel bulb, thinly sliced
3 leeks, cut into discs
a splash of white wine vinegar
1/2 teaspoon caster sugar
3 sprigs of fresh thyme, leaves only
a small knob of butter
Maldon salt
freshly ground black pepper

Preheat the oven to 180°C/gas 4. Put the sausages on a baking tray, prick them and drizzle over a little olive oil. Place in the oven and roast for about 20 minutes, turning them over halfway through.

Meanwhile, coat the bottom of a heavy-based frying pan with olive oil. Add the fennel and leeks and cook on a high heat for about 3 minutes so that they brown slightly. Turn down the heat and add the vinegar and sugar. Mix it all together, then add the thyme and butter. Cook for a further 4–5 minutes or until the vegetables are soft but still retain a little crunch. Season with salt and pepper and serve with the sausages.

Ham simmered in cider with a mustard & parsley sauce

SERVES 4–6 / PREP TIME: 10 MINUTES / COOKING TIME: 1 HOUR

This is a sturdy English meal and absolutely delicious. I like to use a West Country organic cider from Weston's that isn't too dry. Somehow it permeates the skin of the ham as it cooks and makes it slightly sweet and very succulent. Potatoes mashed with parsnips makes a perfect accompaniment, or boiled potatoes and buttery cabbage, with a chilled bottle of amber cider to drink as you tuck in to your meal.

1 piece of ham on the bone, about 1.5kg
100cl bottle of medium cider
1 tablespoon Dijon mustard
a bunch of fresh flat-leaf parsley, finely chopped
Maldon salt
freshly ground black pepper

Put the ham in a saucepan and cover with the cider (you may need more cider, depending on the size of the ham and the pan). Cover the pan and bring to the boil. Simmer gently for up to 1 hour or until the cider has reduced by about one-third and the ham is tender when prodded with a fork.

Add the Dijon mustard and stir well, then let it bubble gently for a few more minutes. Remove the ham and slice thinly. Add the parsley to the cooking liquid and stir in well, then season to taste with salt and pepper. Pour over the ham.

Another idea: Rabbit with verjuice

Melt 4 tablespoons of goose fat in a large heavy-based frying pan and fry 2 rabbits, cut into joints, until golden brown. Add 4 chopped cloves of garlic and cook for a further 2 minutes. Add 300ml chicken stock, 200ml verjuice (available from specialist delis and larger supermarkets) and 4 chicken livers, trimmed and chopped. Season to taste with salt and pepper. Continue to simmer, uncovered, until the rabbit is cooked and the liquid has reduced. Just before serving, sprinkle over 4 tablespoons of chopped fresh flat-leaf parsley.

Fried mustard pork with parsnips & sage

SERVES 2 / PREP TIME: 15 MINUTES / COOKING TIME: 20 MINUTES

This is a perfect winter dish, incorporating ingredients that are all old friends. It definitely needs mashed potato made with tons of butter, to soak up all the mustardy, creamy sauce. The dish leans towards the rustic so I would want to drink a bottle of Normandy cider with it.

2 parsnips, peeled and cut into quarters
2 Cox's apples, cut into quarters and cored
extra virgin olive oil
Maldon salt
1 white onion, chopped
1 large garlic clove, finely chopped
500g pork steak, cut into chunks
3 fresh sage leaves
1/2 tablespoon wholegrain mustard
125ml double cream
freshly ground black pepper
a small bunch of fresh flat-leaf parsley, roughly chopped

Preheat the oven to 190°C/gas 5. Spread out the parsnips and apples on a baking tray. Drizzle over some olive oil and sprinkle with salt. Roast for about 15 minutes or until tender.

Meanwhile, lightly coat the bottom of a large frying pan with olive oil and heat. Add the onion and garlic and sauté until soft. Add the pork and sage leaves and sauté until thoroughly cooked, stirring to brown evenly. Stir in the wholegrain mustard, then stir in the cream. Cook for a few more minutes, stirring, then season generously with salt and pepper and scatter over the parsley. Serve with the apples and parsnips.

Pork & sweet potato mash with ginger, chives & soy

SERVES 2 / PREP TIME: 10 MINUTES / COOKING TIME: 30 MINUTES

Adding ginger to a sweet potato mash lifts the flavour spectacularly and the flicker of green from the chives gives it a lively appearance. Pour all the juice from the pan over the meat and don't throw the bones away if you're one for gnawing.

1 large or 2 small sweet potatoes
1 teaspoon grated fresh ginger
a few fresh chives
Maldon salt
freshly ground black pepper
2 large pork loin chops
1 teaspoon extra virgin olive oil
2 teaspoons soy sauce

Preheat the oven to 200°C/gas 6 and preheat the grill to moderate. Place the sweet potatoes in the oven and bake for about 30 minutes, depending on size. Insert a fork to check if the potatoes are tender. Peel off the skins and mash the ochre interior. Combine it with the ginger and a few snipped chives (reserving a couple for the garnish), then season to taste with salt and pepper.

While the potatoes are baking, lay the chops on a grill pan and drizzle over the olive oil and soy sauce. Grill until the meat is browned on both sides and cooked through, and the fat is crispy. Remove from the grill, reserving the juices in the pan, and slice the meat off the bones. Place the grill pan on top of the cooker and heat up the soy mixture. Toss in the sliced meat and let it cook for a couple of minutes. Put it on hot plates with the mash and pour over the juices. Garnish with a couple of chives and serve immediately, with a green salad.

Another idea: Pork chops with an orange & clove sauce

Make four incisions in the fat on 2 large pork loin chops and insert cloves into each one. Drizzle olive oil over the bottom of a heavy-based frying pan. When the oil is hot brown the chops on both sides, making sure you also brown the fat on the side so it goes crispy. After about 10 minutes of cooking, add a finely chopped clove of garlic and let it become soft. Add the zest and juice of 2 oranges and let it bubble away so that it starts to reduce. When it's becoming thick, add 1 tablespoon of soured cream and stir well. Season to taste with salt and pepper. Throw in 1 tablespoon of finely chopped fresh flat-leaf parsley and serve.

Greek cheeseburger

SERVES 2 / PREP TIME: 15 MINUTES PLUS AT LEAST 10 MINUTES STANDING
COOKING TIME: 10 MINUTES

This is a Greek twist on a cheeseburger – a lamb burger stuffed with feta cheese. Rather than forcing the burger into a pitta bread pocket, cut the pitta bread in half and sandwich the mint leaves and burger in the two halves. Buy some good-quality spicy tomato relish or chutney and spread it on top of the burger, too.

1 slice of day-old white bread, crusts removed
250g lamb mince
1 small red onion, finely chopped
1 garlic clove, crushed
1 teaspoon ground allspice
2 tablespoons chopped fresh flat-leaf parsley
Maldon salt
freshly ground black pepper
125g feta cheese, cubed
extra virgin olive oil
2 pitta breads
a bunch of fresh mint, leaves only

Cut the bread into cubes and soak in a bowl of warm water for a few minutes, then drain and squeeze out any excess moisture. Mix the bread with the minced lamb, onion, garlic, allspice and parsley, and season generously with salt and pepper. Knead together to combine all the ingredients thoroughly. Divide the mixture in half and shape each portion into a burger. Make a hollow in the centre, taking care not to push through to the other side, and stuff in the feta. Leave for about 10 minutes, or up to an hour if you can.

Drizzle olive oil over the bottom of a frying pan and heat. Cook the burgers for about 10 minutes, turning them over halfway through, or until cooked. Serve on the pitta bread with fresh mint leaves.

Another idea: Cumin & lamb meatballs

In a bowl, combine 450g lamb mince, 1 finely chopped red onion and the following fresh herbs, finely chopped: 2 teaspoons of flat-leaf parsley, 1 teaspoon of thyme, 2 sage leaves and 2 cloves of garlic. Season well with salt and pepper. Mix in 1 beaten egg. In the palm of your hand shape the mixture into meatballs, about the size of ping pong balls. Sprinkle plain flour on a board and roll the meatballs over it to coat them.

Coat the bottom of a large frying pan with olive oil. When hot, add the meatballs, in one layer, and sprinkle with 2 teaspoons of ground cumin. Cook over a moderately high heat for about 10 minutes or until browned all over. Serve with fried potatoes and spring greens.

Lamb casserole with quince, thyme & caramelised shallots

SERVES 4–6 / PREP TIME: 20 MINUTES / COOKING TIME: 2 HOURS

Casseroles are my favourite type of cooking. The key is to have wonderfully fresh ingredients, which need the merest amount of coaxing, and to throw them into a casserole dish and let them simmer contentedly away in the oven for a couple of hours. Serve with mashed potato cooked with spring garlic and heaps of extra virgin olive oil and black pepper.

extra virgin olive oil
1.5kg lamb neck fillets, cut into chunks
Maldon salt
1kg shallots, peeled
6 garlic cloves, peeled
a bunch of fresh thyme
150g membrillo (Spanish quince paste)
1 teaspoon vegetable bouillon powder
570ml water
1 teaspoon caster sugar
4 medium to large potatoes, peeled and quartered

Preheat the oven to 180°C/gas 4. Thinly coat the bottom of a large flameproof casserole with olive oil and heat on a high heat. Throw in some of the chunks of lamb – don't crowd them, otherwise they will start to steam – and brown them on all sides. Remove them as soon as they start to brown and do the next batch. Return all the meat to the casserole and season well with salt. Add half of the shallots, the garlic, most of the thyme (keep a couple of sprigs for the garnish), the membrillo, bouillon powder and water. Stir everything together well, then cover and place on the middle shelf of the oven. Cook for about 2 hours, stirring from time to time.

Meanwhile, coat the bottom of a small frying pan with olive oil. Sprinkle over the sugar, then put in the remaining shallots. Cook gently until they are caramelised and tender. Set aside.

About 35 minutes before the lamb has finished cooking, add the potatoes to the casserole. Three minutes before eating add the caramelised shallots and stir them in gently to absorb the heat. Sprinkle the reserved thyme on top and serve.

Lamb chops with warm butternut squash & a black olive dressing

SERVES 2 / PREP TIME: 15 MINUTES / COOKING TIME: 30 MINUTES

I feel it is so important to take advantage of our own seasonal fruit and vegetables. It's food that is at its peak, not forced or from thousands of miles away. Pumpkins and butternut squash, which are full of beneficial beta-carotene, are in season in the UK in mid to late autumn. That's the time to enjoy this dish.

1 butternut squash or small pumpkin, peeled, deseeded and cut into chunks
extra virgin olive oil
Maldon salt
4 fresh bay leaves
2½ teaspoons white wine vinegar
1 teaspoon caster sugar
100g Provençal black olives, pitted and finely chopped
grated zest of 1 lemon
freshly ground black pepper
2–4 lamb loin chops

Preheat the oven to 180°C/gas 4. Place the squash chunks in a roasting tin, drizzle over some olive oil and add a sprinkling of salt. Tuck in two of the bay leaves. Place in the oven and cook for about 20 minutes or until tender, turning the chunks over halfway through the cooking. Remove from the oven and leave to cool slightly.

Preheat the grill to high. In a jam jar or bowl, combine the vinegar and sugar. Add the olives, lemon zest and some pepper. Shake or whisk well. Place the butternut squash in a bowl with the remaining bay leaves. Pour over the dressing and season with salt and pepper.

Brush the lamb chops with olive oil and season with salt. Place them under the grill and cook until they are well browned and the fat is crispy, turning occasionally. Serve immediately with the warm squash salad.

Mustard roast beef with chunky chips

SERVES 4–6 / PREP TIME: 20 MINUTES / COOKING TIME: 55 MINUTES

This beautifully cooked roast topside of beef becomes pinker and pinker in the middle. Cut it wafer thin and serve with crisp chunky chips (have some mayonnaise spiked with a little Tabasco sauce or horseradish for dunking) and a watercress salad. Invest in an excellent bottle of bold Shiraz and get ready for an immensely enjoyable evening.

1/2 teaspoon dry English mustard
1 beef topside joint, about 1.35kg
freshly ground black pepper
sunflower oil, for deep-frying
2kg King Edward potatoes, peeled and chopped into chunky chips
Maldon salt

Preheat the oven to 220°C/gas 7. Rub the dry mustard into the fatty side of the joint, then grind over some pepper. Set the joint in a roasting tin. Place in the oven and roast for 15 minutes, then turn down the heat to 180°C/gas 4. If you like your beef medium rare roast for a further 20 minutes per 450g; for underdone beef roast for 15 minutes per 450g. Let the meat rest for at least 15 minutes before carving.

While the beef is resting, heat the sunflower oil in a deep-sided saucepan over a moderate heat until it shimmers, then fry the chips in small batches until they are crispy, golden and gorgeous. (Always have a damp tea towel at the ready in case of fire in the chip pan.) Drain the chips on kitchen paper and sprinkle them with salt.

Carve the beef wafer thin and serve with the chips and a watercress salad.

Another idea: Grainy mustard & parsley-crusted fillet of beef

Preheat the oven to 220°C/gas 7. In a bowl, mix 6 heaped teaspoons of wholegrain mustard with a large handful of finely chopped fresh flat-leaf parsley until well integrated. Place a 1–1.5kg piece of fillet of beef in a roasting tin. With a palette knife spread the mustard and parsley mixture over the beef like a fine crust. Cover loosely with foil to prevent the crust from cooking, then place in the oven. Roast for 30–35 minutes (this is for very pink beef).

Let the beef rest for about 10 minutes, then slice thinly and arrange on a plate of sliced buttery new potatoes. Serve immediately.

Roast duck with a spice & citrus syrup

SERVES 4-6 / PREP TIME: 15 MINUTES / COOKING TIME: 1¼ HOURS

Duck is fabulous and its meat and fatty skin work well with spices. Serve this with red cabbage cooked with apples, brown sugar, cloves and balsamic vinegar, and celebrate with a bottle of full-bodied claret. Keep the fat from the duck for roasting potatoes. It will keep for a few months in the fridge in a closed container.

1 duck, preferably Gressingham, about 2kg
1 onion, quartered
1 apple, quartered
Maldon salt
1 mace blade
1 teaspoon cloves
1 star anise
1 cinnamon stick
4 teaspoons runny honey
500ml cream sherry
2 bay leaves
3 strips of lemon zest
3 strips of orange zest

Preheat the oven to 190°C/gas 5. Remove any giblets from the duck and put the onion and apple into the body cavity. Score the breast of the duck, cutting into the fat but not through to the flesh, and rub salt into the skin. Place the duck breast side down on a rack in a roasting tin. Roast for about 1 hour or until cooked. During roasting pour off the excess fat from the tin. About 25 minutes before the end of the roasting time, turn the duck breast side up.

Meanwhile, make the spice syrup. Combine the mace, cloves, star anise, cinnamon, honey, sherry, bay leaves and lemon and orange zests in a saucepan. Gently bring to the boil, then simmer until reduced to a syrup. Taste and stir in more honey if you prefer it sweeter. Strain the syrup into a jug.

Transfer the duck to a serving platter and serve with the syrup.

Another idea: Guinea fowl with caramelised kumquats & bay leaves

Preheat the oven to 180°C/gas 4. Place 1 large guinea fowl (about 1.5kg) in a roasting tin and scatter 250g kumquats around it. Crush 6 fresh bay leaves in your hand to release the flavour, then place them among the kumquats. Liberally drizzle with extra virgin olive oil and sprinkle generously with salt. Put in the oven to roast for about 40 minutes or until the juices run clear.

Remove the guinea fowl, pouring the juices out of the bird into the tin, and place it on a plate with the kumquats. Rest in a warm place for 10 minutes. Set the roasting tin on the cooker and simmer the juices, mixing in the sticky bits to make a gravy. Carve the bird and serve with the kumquats and gravy.

Acorn squash with lemon, garlic, bacon & parsley

SERVES 1 (DOUBLE, TRIPLE AND SO ON, ACCORDING TO HOW MANY YOU ARE SERVING)

PREP TIME: 10 MINUTES / COOKING TIME: 40 MINUTES

Acorn squash are not as sweet as pumpkin or sweet potato, but cooking them this way the garlic, lemon and oil melt into the flesh, making it all gooey. The squash looks beautiful on presentation and it's fun lifting the lid. The seeds of the squash can be dried, painted and made into necklaces if you are so inclined.

1 small acorn squash
2 tablespoons extra virgin olive oil
juice of 1/2 lemon
2 garlic cloves, crushed
Maldon salt
freshly ground black pepper
2–4 bacon rashers
a small handful of fresh flat-leaf parsley leaves, finely chopped

Preheat the oven to 200°C/gas 6. Cut the top off the squash and scoop out the seeds and fibres. Add the olive oil, lemon juice and garlic to the hollow in the squash and season generously with salt and pepper. Put the lid back on and set in a deep roasting tin. Put enough water into the tin to come halfway up the side of the squash. Place in the oven and cook for about 40 minutes or until the flesh of the squash is soft.

Fry or grill the bacon until it is crispy, then chop into pieces. When the squash is ready insert the pieces of bacon and sprinkle with parsley, then put the lid back on and serve.

Brussels sprouts with prosciutto & thyme

SERVES 1-2 / PREP TIME: 15 MINUTES / COOKING TIME: 15 MINUTES

If you give Brussels sprouts a little TLC they become a deeply satisfying vegetable and enhance other ingredients cooked alongside. Serve this with good bread or, if you have more time, a baked potato topped with a large dollop of unsalted butter and a few more fresh thyme leaves. I think a pint of draught Guinness is the perfect drink for a comfort dinner like this.

170g small Brussels sprouts, outer leaves removed
extra virgin olive oil
1 small red onion, finely chopped
10g unsalted butter
a small handful of fresh thyme leaves
3 slices of prosciutto, cut into thin strips
Maldon salt
freshly ground black pepper

Cut a cross in the base of each sprout, then steam them until tender.

Meanwhile, drizzle some olive oil in a large frying pan and heat. Sauté the onion until soft. Add the butter and let everything start to sizzle, then add the sprouts and thyme leaves. Cook until the sprouts are beginning to brown. Stir in the strips of prosciutto and cook for a few minutes more. Season to taste with salt and pepper and serve immediately.

Another idea: Corned beef with mustard sauce & Savoy cabbage

Put 100ml dry white wine in a saucepan, add 1 finely chopped shallot and cook over a high heat until the liquid has reduced to about 1½ tablespoons. Add 100ml vegetable stock and simmer until it has slightly reduced. Turn down the heat, then stir in 100ml double cream and season with salt and pepper. Simmer on a low heat for 7–10 minutes, then stir in 2 teaspoons of wholegrain mustard.

While the sauce is simmering, steam a small shredded Savoy cabbage until al dente. Return it to the saucepan with a large knob of unsalted butter and season well. Slice the corned beef into thin slices and divide them between two plates. Pour over the mustard sauce and serve with the hot cabbage.

five

friends for supper – delicious easy dinners

A pile of seafood with samphire, shallots & parsley

SERVES 4–6 / PREP TIME: 25–30 MINUTES / COOKING TIME: ABOUT 10 MINUTES

Samphire is a sort of sea asparagus and turns up seasonally at more or less the same time as its earthborn counterpart. From about May to August this precious sea vegetable, with its salty iodine flavour, appears in wooden boxes at more select fishmongers. It's incredibly pretty, looking like verdant green coral. It goes without saying that samphire accompanies fish very well. Although it might seem undignified having a pile of seafood, it's a rather fun lottery and every part of the 'pile' is more than worthy. Serve this with boiled Jersey Royal potatoes tossed with chopped fresh mint, butter and seasoning.

200ml dry white wine
3 garlic cloves, peeled
6 fresh bay leaves
400g red mullet fillets, skin scaled
6 raw large prawns, peeled and butterflied (see page 39)
300g fresh clams in shell, scrubbed
6 scallops, shelled

Sauce
150g unsalted butter
2 small shallots, finely chopped
330g samphire
a handful of fresh flat-leaf parsley leaves, finely chopped

Put the wine, garlic and bay leaves in the bottom of a large steamer and bring to simmering point. Carefully lay out all the fish and shellfish on the steamer rack, set over the simmering liquid and cover. Steam for 3–4 minutes. Make sure the scallops and fish are just cooked, the prawns have turned pink and the clams have opened (discard any that haven't).

Meanwhile, gently melt the butter in a saucepan and cook the shallots until softened. Add the samphire and cook for a further 3–4 minutes. When ready, stir in the parsley until well integrated and warm.

Pile the seafood in a serving dish, spoon over the samphire sauce and serve.

Crayfish tails in parsley butter with new potatoes, shallots & pimentón

SERVES 4 / PREP TIME: 10 MINUTES / COOKING TIME: 30 MINUTES

Crayfish are the freshwater counterparts of the marine lobster. They are available in some fishmongers and larger supermarkets. Lobster tails will work just as well in this recipe, but are probably pricier. You'll find pimentón in Spanish delis or Asian corner shops. It's a sweeter, less spicy version of paprika that is commonly used in Spain.

1kg new potatoes
extra virgin olive oil
400g shallots, peeled
2 large pinches of pimentón
2 teaspoons caster sugar
200g unsalted butter, at room temperature
a handful of fresh flat-leaf parsley leaves, roughly chopped
400g cooked crayfish tails
Maldon salt
freshly ground black pepper

Cook the potatoes in plenty of boiling salted water until al dente.

Meanwhile, heat a drizzle of olive oil in a frying pan, lay in the shallots and sprinkle with the pimentón and sugar. Cook on a moderate heat until tender. When the potatoes are ready, drain them and add them to the shallots. Turn up the heat and brown them a little.

In a bowl, mash the butter with the parsley. Melt the parsley butter in another frying pan. When it's gently bubbling stir in the crayfish tails and warm through. Season to taste with salt and pepper. Serve with the potatoes.

Whole snapper with galangal, teriyaki, spring onion & holy basil

SERVES 4–6 / PREP TIME: 12 MINUTES / COOKING TIME: 15 MINUTES

I find it immensely satisfying baking a fish in its entirety for supper – serving it whole, sizzling and juicy from the oven, always brings a sense of ceremony to the table. The holy basil used in this dish is grown in Thailand and other Asian countries; available from most Asian food shops, its flavour is a little more perfumed than Mediterranean basil and the leaves a little spikier. Galangal, which is Thai ginger, is slightly less strong than our normal fresh root ginger and so can be used in larger quantities than the amount of ginger you might normally add to a recipe. Galangal is available in any Asian or Chinese supermarket.

1 snapper or sea bass, about 1.2kg, scaled and cleaned
8 teaspoons teriyaki sauce
6 teaspoons shredded fresh galangal
5 spring onions, green part only, shredded
a small bunch of fresh holy basil, leaves only

Preheat the oven to 180°C/gas 4. Cut two slits on each side of the fish. In a bowl, combine the teriyaki sauce with 2 teaspoons of the shredded galangal to make a marinade. Put another 2 teaspoons of galangal and half of the spring onions in the cavity of the fish. Brush the snapper on both sides with the marinade and place in a roasting dish. Put in the oven and bake for about 15 minutes or until cooked (test with a fork, which should go in easily).

Remove from the oven and transfer to a serving dish. Sprinkle over the rest of the galangal and spring onions and the holy basil leaves. Serve immediately with steamed spring greens and the juices from the fish.

Salt cod & potato casserole with olives

SERVES 4–6 / PREP TIME: 2 HOURS OFF AND ON, PLUS SOAKING THE COD IN WATER FOR 24 HOURS / COOKING TIME: 40 MINUTES

It's said that a salt merchant from Oporto in Portugal first created this dish, which is called *Bacalhau à Gomes de Sá* in Portuguese. Soaking the cod in milk softens it. The recipe works particularly well when cooked in a terracotta dish, so invest in one if you haven't already got one. They are good value and also look great served directly on the table.

500g salted cod
300ml milk
850g potatoes, scrubbed
120ml extra virgin olive oil
2 onions, thinly sliced into rings
2 garlic cloves, crushed
3 medium eggs, hard boiled and sliced
100g Spanish black olives
a small bunch of fresh flat-leaf parsley, leaves only
Maldon salt
freshly ground black pepper

Soak the cod in a bowl of cold water in the fridge for 24 hours, changing the water frequently. Drain well, then put the cod in a pan. Pour over enough boiling water to cover it and leave to soak for 30 minutes, covered to keep hot.

Drain the cod, then remove the skin and bones, keeping the flesh as intact as possible. Place the fish in a heatproof bowl. Heat the milk in a saucepan to the brink of boiling, then pour it over the fish. Cover and let it stand for 1 hour. Meanwhile, cook the potatoes in boiling salted water until tender; drain, then peel and slice.

Preheat the oven to 200°C/gas 6. Drain the fish well, then flake it. Heat the olive oil in a large frying pan and sauté the onions and garlic until soft. Add the potatoes and flaked cod. Season to taste with salt and pepper, then cook over a low heat, turning the ingredients occasionally, for about 10 minutes without allowing them to fry. Transfer to a terracotta dish and bake on the top shelf of the oven for about 15 minutes or until golden.

Lay the eggs, olives and parsley on top, drizzle with a little more olive oil, season and serve immediately.

Mint & chive risotto with seared scallops

SERVES 4–6 / PREP TIME: 10 MINUTES / COOKING TIME: 20 MINUTES

What I find enjoyable about this dish is that by adding the scallops to the risotto it gives the dish a sense of grandeur. The downside of making risotto is that you have to be hovering next to the cooker, as it can't be left. But there really is only the prepping to do, so there isn't much sweating in the kitchen beforehand.

extra virgin olive oil
7 spring onions, cut into discs
1/4 fresh garlic bulb, cloves finely chopped
a small glass of dry white wine
500g risotto rice (Arborio or Carnaroli)
about 1.5 litres vegetable stock, hot
80g Parmesan, freshly grated
Maldon salt
freshly ground black pepper
a knob of unsalted butter
12–18 scallops, removed from the shell
a handful of fresh mint leaves, finely chopped
a handful of fresh chives, snipped

Coat the bottom of a large, heavy-based saucepan with olive oil. When the oil is hot, add the spring onions and garlic and cook until soft. Pour in the wine and let it evaporate. Add the rice and stir it into the oily mixture. When you feel it beginning to catch on the bottom, pour in a ladle of hot stock. Keep stirring until the rice catches again, then add another ladleful of stock. Repeat until the rice is al dente. Stir in half the grated cheese and season to taste with salt and pepper. Add the butter and then the remaining grated cheese. Cover and keep warm.

Drizzle some olive oil over the bottom of a frying pan and heat it over a high heat, then add the scallops and sear for about 1 minute on each side.

Place the risotto in a hot serving dish. Arrange the scallops on top and sprinkle over the mint and chives. Serve immediately.

Hanoi fishcakes with mint, coriander & lime

SERVES 4 / PREP TIME: 17 MINUTES / COOKING TIME: ABOUT 8 MINUTES

Of all the Asian cuisines, Vietnamese is my favourite. As you would expect, it has similarities to Thai and Malaysian cooking, and it is as delicate and feminine as a shutsong (a traditional Vietnamese woman's costume). For fishcakes like these, the Vietnamese would use a white fish such as John Dory or snapper, both of which are easy to find here, and they would add lots of fresh herbs. Lime, mint and coriander work really well together and still manage to retain their individual tastes. I just squeeze lime over the fishcakes, but if you want a dipping sauce you can buy one from your local Asian supermarket. It's good to have a bottle in the storecupboard for regular use.

2 garlic cloves, peeled
4 spring onions
1 large red chilli, deseeded
12 fresh mint leaves
a handful of fresh coriander leaves
4 teaspoons fish sauce
600g John Dory or snapper fillets, skinned
plain flour for coating
vegetable oil for frying
4 fresh limes, cut into wedges

Combine the garlic, spring onions, chilli, mint and coriander leaves in a food processor and blitz to a thick paste. Add the fish sauce and blitz to mix. Transfer to a bowl. Put the fish in the food processor and grind to a coarse paste. Add the fish to the bowl and mix with the spicy herb paste. Shape into four cakes and coat with flour.

Coat the bottom of a medium frying pan with oil and heat. When the oil is hot add the fishcakes and fry for about 8 minutes or until golden brown on both sides. Serve immediately, with lime wedges and steamed jasmine rice.

Salt & parsley-crusted sea bass

SERVES 4–6 / PREP TIME: 10 MINUTES PLUS 5 MINUTES STANDING
COOKING TIME: ABOUT 35 MINUTES

This is a beautiful and mysterious dish. When you present it at the table your guests will definitely be impressed. For me it's always an exciting moment when you break off the blanket of salt to reveal the succulent fish beneath. You'll find that the salt will take off the skin of the fish so it's important to stress to the fishmonger to leave the scales on. There are no rules about what to put in the cavity, but I favour slices of citrus fruit and fennel. Instead of serving potatoes or rice with this fish, try spaghetti or linguini drizzled with a fine Tuscan extra virgin olive oil, some lemon juice and finely chopped fresh flat-leaf parsley. Snapper also works very well baked in a salt crust.

2kg rock salt or Maldon salt
500ml water
1 sea bass, about 2kg, scales left on and cleaned
1 small fennel bulb, thinly sliced
6 lemon slices
a small bunch of fresh flat-leaf parsley, finely chopped
extra virgin olive oil

Preheat the oven to 220°C/gas 7. Put the salt and water in a bowl and mix together. Fill the cavity of the fish with the fennel and lemon slices, then place the fish on a baking tray oiled with a little olive oil. Sprinkle the parsley on top of the fish. Cover the fish with the salt paste, patting it firmly all over. If you do not have enough salt, leave the head uncovered. Bake for 35 minutes.

Allow to stand for about 5 minutes, then take to the table, remove the salt crust, brushing away any remaining salt, and serve.

Grilled sea bass fillets with potato & courgette gratin

SERVES 4–6 / PREP TIME: 10 MINUTES / COOKING TIME: 35–40 MINUTES

All the effort in this dish goes into the making of the gratin. Firstly you have to boil the potatoes, then sauté the courgettes with parsley and garlic, and then make a white sauce. By comparison, the fish is a doddle to deal with. I urge you to buy it already filleted, unless you are proficient at cleaning fish. The lemon slices on the fish look good and the juice seeps in subtly, making the fish really delicious.

4 medium potatoes, scrubbed
140g unsalted butter, plus extra for greasing
4 tablespoons plain flour
Maldon salt
1 litre milk, warmed
extra virgin olive oil
4 medium courgettes, thinly sliced
3 garlic cloves, crushed
1 tablespoon finely chopped fresh flat-leaf parsley
4–6 sea bass or John Dory fillets, about 200g each
3 lemons, sliced

Cook the potatoes in boiling salted water until almost tender. Drain and peel off the skins. Allow to cool, then slice.

While the potatoes are cooking, melt 125g of the butter in a saucepan. Stir in the flour with a wooden spoon, then add a generous pinch of salt and mix over a moderate heat until smooth. Slowly add the warm milk, stirring constantly until the sauce has thickened. Turn down the heat to very low and leave the sauce to simmer gently, stirring occasionally.

Preheat the grill to high. Coat the bottom of a large frying pan with olive oil and add the remaining butter. When sizzling, throw in the courgettes and cook for a few minutes. Add the garlic and parsley and cook for a further few minutes, making sure the courgettes do not turn brown. Season well with salt.

Grease an ovenproof dish with butter and put the potatoes in the dish. Add the courgettes (if you are a perfectionist go for layering), then cover with the white sauce. Put under the grill for about 5 minutes or until the top is brown. Keep the gratin hot.

Brush the fillets with olive oil and add a good pinch of salt, then place under the grill and cook for 3–4 minutes on each side. Arrange the lemon slices on top of the fish, and serve with the gratin.

Penne with roasted vine tomatoes & pancetta

SERVES 4 / PREP TIME: 10 MINUTES / COOKING TIME: 35–40 MINUTES

I like the Italian bacon called pancetta rather than our own processed, packaged bacon; when you fry or grill the thin strips, the fat becomes golden and crispy, and it literally melts in your mouth. The acid sweetness of the roasted tomatoes in this dish works gloriously with the salty harshness of the pancetta. Combine these ingredients with fresh Parmesan, softened and sticky red onions, extra virgin olive oil and garlic, and use to coat pasta cooked al dente, and you have a delicious, simple dinner. If there's a bottle of Chianti lounging around, crack it open. After such a filling meal, I'd advise leaving the washing-up until morning.

1.1kg vine-ripened cherry tomatoes
extra virgin olive oil
20 thin slices of pancetta
2 large red onions, finely chopped
6 garlic cloves, finely chopped
200g Parmesan, freshly grated
500g penne
Maldon salt
freshly ground black pepper

Preheat the oven to 180°C/gas 4. Place the tomatoes, still attached to the vine, in a roasting dish and drizzle with olive oil. Roast for 20–25 minutes or until they are slightly brown and squishy.

Meanwhile, lay the pancetta slices in a large frying pan, without any oil (the pancetta will release a lot of fat while cooking), and cook until crispy. Remove and put aside; when cool break into pieces. If there is not sufficient pancetta fat left in the pan, add a drizzle of olive oil, then add the onions and garlic and cook until soft. Do not let the garlic get brown, as this will make the dish bitter.

Remove the roasted tomatoes from the vine and add them to the frying pan. Add the pancetta, too. With a wooden spoon squash the tomatoes and stir them into the other ingredients. Bring to simmering point and cook for a few minutes before stirring in two-thirds of the Parmesan until melted.

While the sauce is being made, cook the penne in a large pan of boiling salted water as per the packet instructions, until al dente. Drain and return to the pan. Pour over the sauce and return to a moderate heat. Stir until the pasta is well amalgamated with the sauce, then put it into a hot serving dish and sprinkle with the remaining Parmesan and some pepper. Taste before adding any salt. Serve immediately.

Merguez sausages on rosemary sticks with a beetroot, Greek yogurt & mint salad

SERVES 4–6 / PREP TIME: 15 MINUTES PLUS ABOUT 1 HOUR FOR COOKING THE BEETROOTS
COOKING TIME: 20 MINUTES

Merguez are traditional sausages from North Africa, usually made with lamb, garlic, paprika and fennel seeds. I like to barbecue or roast them on rosemary sticks. I think you need a side dish that will counterbalance the spiciness of the sausages, and this beetroot salad with Greek yogurt and mint should cool your mouth down. (To remove beetroot stains from your hands rub them with a raw potato.) While you are cooking and your friends are hanging around, put out a big bowl of guacamole with blue corn chips for dipping into it.

6 small to medium beetroots
200g Greek yogurt
1 garlic clove, crushed
extra virgin olive oil
Maldon salt
freshly ground black pepper
a handful of fresh mint leaves, roughly chopped
12 woody rosemary stalks
12 merguez sausages

Preheat the oven to 190°C/gas 5. Put the beetroots in an ovenproof dish and bake for about 1 hour or until tender. Allow to cool, then peel and cut into slices.

Lay the beetroot slices in a serving dish. In a small bowl, combine the yogurt, garlic, a drizzle of olive oil, salt and pepper, and mix well. Spoon the mixture over the beetroot and scatter on the mint leaves.

Preheat the barbecue (or turn the oven to 150°C/gas 2). Remove two-thirds of the leaves from the rosemary stalks, leaving a small bunch at the top end. Impale each sausage on a rosemary skewer. Place on the barbecue and cook for about 20 minutes, turning regularly. Or put the sausages on a roasting tray with a dash of olive oil and roast for about 20 minutes, depending on the size of the sausages. Serve with the beetroot salad.

Chorizo baked with apples, rosemary, red onions & potatoes

SERVES 4 / PREP TIME: 15 MINUTES / COOKING TIME: 40 MINUTES

This is one of my favourite kinds of recipes – no weights and measures, just some good ingredients given a little prep time and then left to cook. You can throw the food together, give it a nod and a wink, then shut the oven door, walk away and catch up with your friends. Twenty minutes later, dinner's ready. This just shows that good food doesn't have to be complicated. Chorizo does vary quite a lot. If your tastebuds are Teflon-coated, go for the hot one. I don't like my mouth becoming a furnace, so I tend to go for the mild chorizo or mix hot and mild. On the drink front a cool glass of cider will do the trick.

extra virgin olive oil
8 medium floury potatoes, peeled and diced
8 garlic cloves, peeled
2 red onions, sliced into half moons
2 mild (or hot) chorizo sausages, about 400g, cut into discs
a couple of large sprigs of fresh rosemary
Maldon salt
2 large Cox's apples, peeled, quartered and cored

Preheat the oven to 200°C/gas 6. Liberally coat the bottom of a roasting dish with olive oil and place it in the oven. By the time you've prepared all of the other ingredients the oil should be hot. Carefully add the potatoes, garlic, onions, chorizo and rosemary to the dish and sprinkle with salt. Turn all the ingredients until they are well coated with oil, then spread them out evenly. Put the dish back in the oven and bake for 20 minutes.

Chuck in the apple quarters and bake for another 20 minutes. This is a dish that you can overcook quite happily; it's up to you how brown and crispy you want the potatoes to be.

Chorizo & parsley potato cakes with saffron & paprika aïoli

SERVES 4–6 / PREP TIME: 35 MINUTES / COOKING TIME: 10 MINUTES

These are a meat version of fishcakes. I prefer a milder chorizo, but you could use a combination of mild and hot. If you feel like having another vegetable, Kenyan green beans cooked al dente would be delicious, and if you want a salad toss lamb's lettuce with a little olive oil and salt.

3 mild cooking chorizo sausages, about 450g in total
6 floury potatoes, peeled
40g unsalted butter
3 medium eggs
1½ tablespoons finely chopped fresh flat-leaf parsley
plain flour
extra virgin olive oil

Aïoli
2 garlic cloves, peeled
2 medium egg yolks, at room temperature, beaten
300ml extra virgin olive oil, at room temperature
a pinch of saffron threads
a pinch of paprika
Maldon salt
a squeeze of lemon juice
freshly ground black pepper

To make the aïoli, pound the garlic in a large mortar until it's a little paste-like. Mix in the egg yolks, then literally drop by drop add the olive oil, whisking until you have a thick consistency. Pinch in the saffron with the paprika and some salt. Add the lemon juice and pepper to taste and stir well. Set aside.

Preheat the oven to 200°C/gas 6. Put the chorizo in a roasting dish and roast for about 20 minutes or until cooked. Allow to cool, then chop roughly. While the chorizo is roasting, cook the potatoes in plenty of boiling salted water until tender when pricked with a fork. Drain well and return them to the pan. Add the butter and mash until smooth. Allow to cool.

Whisk the eggs with the chopped parsley, salt and pepper in a mixing bowl. When the potatoes are cool enough to handle, stir them into the egg mixture with the chorizo. Combine well. Dust a wooden board or work surface with flour. Take a large spoonful of the potato mixture and form into a ball (burger size). Flatten on the board and coat both sides lightly with flour. Continue making the cakes until you have required number.

Coat the bottom of a frying pan with olive oil. When hot, put in the cakes in one layer, without them touching each other. Cook for about 10 minutes or until crispy and golden on both sides. Serve immediately with the aïoli.

Thai chicken & coconut soup

SERVES 4 / PREP TIME: 12 MINUTES / COOKING TIME: 25–30 MINUTES

Coconut soup has to be one of my favourite Asian dishes. It is very much a meal in itself, full of delicious ingredients that can be supplemented or replaced as you like. If you don't feel like having it too spicy hold back on the chillies. Add more coriander or lime if your tastebuds go in that direction, and use a handful of raw medium-sized prawns if you don't like chicken.

2 chicken breasts
4 stalks of lemongrass, finely chopped
4 shallots, finely chopped
2 garlic cloves, peeled
6 kaffir lime leaves
1 red chilli, deseeded and finely chopped, plus sliced red chilli to garnish
800ml coconut milk
800ml chicken stock
2 tablespoons fish sauce
4 teaspoons caster sugar
80g coconut cream
a handful of beansprouts
4 teaspoons grated fresh ginger
a small handful fresh coriander leaves
4 lime wedges

Preheat the grill to moderate. Grill the chicken breasts for 10–15 minutes or until they are cooked through. Cool slightly, then finely chop the meat, discarding the skin and bone.

While the chicken is cooking, pound the lemongrass with the shallots, garlic, lime leaves and chopped chilli in a mortar. Combine the coconut milk, chicken stock and fish sauce in a saucepan and gently bring to simmering point. Add the lemongrass mixture to the stock together with the sugar and let it cook for a few minutes.

Add the chicken and simmer for 5 minutes, then stir in the coconut cream. Cook for a few more minutes. Ladle into bowls, add the beansprouts and ginger, and garnish with sliced chilli and coriander leaves. Serve with the lime wedges to squeeze over.

Chicken chunks with a saffron & basil sauce

SERVES 4 / PREP TIME: 10 MINUTES / COOKING TIME: 30 MINUTES

This is an extremely pretty dish to look at and it tastes very good, too. The friends you are having over for dinner will think that you've really brushed up on your culinary skills. Serve it with buttery new potatoes and open a chilled bottle of delicious Sancerre.

200g unsalted butter
6 shallots, finely chopped
6 garlic cloves, finely chopped
a large pinch of saffron threads
Maldon salt
3 tablespoons double cream
a large bunch of fresh basil, leaves only, finely shredded
extra virgin olive oil
1kg boneless chicken breast, skinned and cut into chunks
freshly ground black pepper

Melt the butter in a frying pan and gently sauté the shallots and garlic until soft. Mix the saffron and a pinch of salt together and add to the pan. Let the saffron yellow bleed out, then stir in the cream. Add the basil. Remove from the heat and set aside.

Coat the bottom of another frying pan with olive oil. When it is hot, brown the chunks of chicken, in batches if necessary. Season with salt and pepper. When they are cooked, use a slotted spoon to transfer them to the basil and saffron mixture. Cook for a minute or two more, then check the seasoning and serve immediately.

Spring poussins with butter, tarragon, pancetta & fried onions

SERVES 4 / PREP TIME: 10 MINUTES / COOKING TIME: 30 MINUTES

I always feel a little bit grand having my own small chicken to eat – you get to enjoy all the different parts, from the breast to the leg to the wing. Tarragon is one of my favourite herbs with chicken. Scoring inside the cavity of the bird allows the aroma of the herb to permeate through the flesh. The longer you leave it stuffed before cooking, the stronger the taste of tarragon will be. If you prefer, you can use rosemary instead of tarragon. I suggest an Italian light white wine and a salad of radicchio alongside.

4 poussins
a large bunch of fresh tarragon
200g unsalted butter, at room temperature
Maldon salt
12 pancetta slices
2 red onions, sliced into rings

Preheat the oven to 190°C/gas 5. With a sharp knife score inside the top of the cavity in each poussin. Stuff with tarragon. Smear the top of the birds with butter and sprinkle with salt. Place on a baking tray. Roast for about 30 minutes. To check if the poussins are cooked, insert a knife between the wing and body; if the juices run clear the poussins are done.

While the poussins are roasting, heat a frying pan, then fry the pancetta until crispy. Remove and reserve. Add the onion rings and sauté in the fat from the pancetta until golden. Serve the pancetta and onions with the poussins.

Another idea: Roast poussin stuffed with fresh garlic

Preheat the oven to 200°C/gas 6. Place 4 fresh garlic bulbs in a small ovenproof dish and sprinkle with salt and a few drops of extra virgin olive oil. Bake for about 20 minutes or until the garlic is soft. Put 1 whole garlic bulb inside each poussin. Brush the outside of the birds with olive oil and sprinkle with salt. Put them in a roasting dish and roast for 35–40 minutes or until the juices run clear.

You can remove the garlic from inside the bird and squidge out the creamy pungent interior to eat with the meat. Serve with chopped tomato mixed with a little chopped fresh flat-leaf parsley, salt and freshly ground black pepper, olive oil and lemon juice. If you like rice, add that to the tomato.

Roast quail with pomegranate, mint & parsley in Greek yogurt

SERVES 4 / PREP TIME: 15 MINUTES / COOKING TIME: 15-20 MINUTES

One of the upsides of the winter months is that we get a few wonderful ingredients, such as pomegranates, which arrive from Persia. Serve the quail with basmati rice, adding some more pomegranate seeds plus fresh mint and chives. If you are extra hungry, do two quails per person.

400g Greek yogurt
a bunch of fresh flat-leaf parsley, leaves only, finely chopped
a bunch of fresh coriander, leaves only, finely chopped
a large bunch of fresh mint, leaves only, finely chopped
Maldon salt
freshly ground black pepper
2 small pomegranates, seeds only
4–8 quails, at room temperature
4 small knobs of butter
extra virgin olive oil

Preheat the oven to 190°C/gas 5. In a mixing bowl, combine the yogurt with the parsley, coriander and half of the mint. Season well with salt and pepper. Stir in the pomegranate seeds but only superficially so that they stay more on the surface and you can appreciate their colour. Set aside.

Stuff each quail with a small knob of butter and the remaining mint. Place in a roasting tin. Drizzle with olive oil and sprinkle with salt. Place in the oven and roast for 15–20 minutes; you want the meat to remain juicy but not pink. Baste with the juices in the tin after about 10 minutes. When ready, serve with the juices and the yogurt sauce.

Fillet of beef with a roast plum tomato dressing

SERVES 4 / PREP TIME: 7 MINUTES PLUS RESTING THE BEEF / COOKING TIME: 30 MINUTES

Roasting the tomatoes for this dressing adds a lovely richness that goes really well with beef. You can either serve the beef warm or cook it the day before so that it is really cold. Accompany this dish with a fresh, crisp green salad and a lovely glass of deep, rich red wine.

8 Roma or plum tomatoes, cut in half
extra virgin olive oil
Maldon salt
1 teaspoon caster sugar
a bunch of fresh chives, snipped
freshly ground black pepper
800g piece of fillet of beef

Preheat the oven to 200°C/gas 6. Lay out the tomatoes on a roasting tray. Drizzle over some olive oil and sprinkle with salt and the sugar. Roast for about 15 minutes or until the tomatoes are soft and mushy. Remove the tomatoes and push them through a sieve. Add 3 tablespoons of olive oil, the chives and salt and pepper, and stir well.

Drizzle olive oil over the bottom of a heavy-based frying pan. When it is hot, fry the fillet of beef for about 15–20 minutes, or longer if you don't like it too pink. Leave it to cool down for 15 minutes or so, then cut it into slices. Place the sliced beef on a serving platter with the tomato dressing on the side.

Lamb shanks with a red pepper & rosemary sauce

SERVES 4–6 / PREP TIME: 40 MINUTES / COOKING TIME: 1½ HOURS

This red pepper sauce has a delicious rich, sweet flavour that rejoices with lamb, making the dish perfect for late summer or autumn. Meat cooked this way has a delightful velvety quality. Serve with garlicky mashed potato (throw in whole cloves of garlic to boil with the potatoes, then mash with plenty of butter and milk), and try a full-bodied red wine from the Sangiovese grape.

4 red onions, quartered
4 garlic cloves, finely sliced
4 sprigs of fresh thyme
6 lamb shanks
extra virgin olive oil
Maldon salt

Sauce
12 firm red peppers
a few sprigs of fresh rosemary, leaves only
freshly ground black pepper

Preheat the oven to 180°C/gas 4. Make a bed of the onions, garlic and thyme in a large, preferably terracotta roasting dish. Put the lamb shanks on top, drizzle over some olive oil and sprinkle with salt. Place in the oven and cook for 1 hour.

Meanwhile, for the pepper sauce, hold each pepper with kitchen tongs over a gas ring on max, turning the pepper as it blackens and chars all over. Alternatively, char the peppers under a preheated hot grill. Put the peppers in a brown paper bag to cool. They will steam gently inside the bag, making them easier to peel.

When the peppers are cool, pull off their charred skins. Rinse and dry well, then slice them in half and remove the cores and seeds. Cut the flesh into strips and lay them in a roasting tin. Drizzle with olive oil, sprinkle with a good pinch of salt and scatter over the rosemary leaves. Put the peppers into the oven with the lamb and roast for at least 30 minutes or until soft. When cool, put them in a food processor with all of the oil from the roasting tin and pulse until smooth. Season to taste with salt and pepper.

Cover the lamb shanks with the pepper sauce, then cook for a further 30 minutes or until the meat falls away from the bones when touched. Serve immediately with garlicky mash or baby baked potatoes.

Breast of duck with couscous, fresh apricots, mint, coriander & red onions

SERVES 4–6 / PREP TIME: 15 MINUTES / COOKING TIME: 30 MINUTES

There are so many ways to cook 'Donald' (as my children like to call duck). This recipe uses only the breasts, so it doesn't take too long; it also means that everyone gets the best bit of the bird. Fresh apricots are delicious roasted – this is a great way to enjoy those that aren't so sweet, as roasting gives them a lovely slightly sweet and sour edge. They go very well with the duck and couscous. Serve this colourful dish on a huge platter in the centre of the table so everyone can help themselves. A watercress salad is delicious alongside; use fresh orange juice instead of lemon juice in the dressing.

4–6 duck breasts
Maldon salt
extra virgin olive oil
7 fresh apricots, cut in half and stoned
6 garlic cloves, whole in their skins
2 large red onions, sliced into half moons
a large handful of fresh mint leaves, roughly chopped
a large handful of fresh coriander leaves, roughly chopped

Couscous
700g couscous
a large knob of unsalted butter
freshly ground black pepper
3 fresh apricots, stoned and cut into chunks

Preheat the oven to 200°C/gas 6. Score the skin on the duck breasts, cutting through the fat but not into the flesh. Make a paste of salt and olive oil and spread thinly over the skin. Arrange the breasts in a roasting tin and scatter the halved apricots and garlic around them. Place in the oven and roast for 20 minutes. Add the onions and roast for a further 10 minutes or until the duck looks crispy and golden.

Meanwhile, cook the couscous as per the packet instructions. Mix in the butter and season to taste with salt and pepper, then pile the hot couscous on a large serving dish. Add the roast and raw apricots and the roast onions. Peel the cooked garlic cloves and toss them into the couscous. Remove the duck breasts to a chopping board and carve thinly. Arrange the duck over the couscous and scatter the mint and coriander on top. Serve immediately.

six

sunday lunch – good food for friends and family

Garlic & lemon prawns with Spanish rice

SERVES 4–6 / PREP TIME: 20 MINUTES / COOKING TIME: ABOUT 20 MINUTES

This dish will definitely bring back happy memories of summer holidays in the Mediterranean. The Spanish rice to look for is Calasparra; it's not as starchy as risotto rice and is used in paella. Have a glorious pile of green lettuces on the side. I love to mop the juices of my meal with dressed salad leaves; I've never been one for a separate bowl for salad. And to drink, try a delicious Spanish white wine called Albarino, which has a hint of sparkle.

500g Spanish Calasparra rice
1.25 litres vegetable stock
extra virgin olive oil
2 garlic bulbs, cloves finely chopped
1kg peeled raw prawns
Maldon salt
juice of 2 large lemons
freshly ground black pepper
a large handful of fresh flat-leaf parsley leaves, roughly chopped

Cook the rice in the vegetable stock for about 18 minutes or until tender.

Meanwhile, heat a generous swirl of olive oil in a large heavy-based frying pan. Add the garlic and let it sizzle away, but do not let it get brown (as this makes it taste bitter). Throw in the prawns and stir as they cook, turning a gorgeous pink. Toss in a hearty pinch of salt and squeeze over the lemon juice. Let all the flavours merge together, shaking the pan constantly. When the prawns are cooked, which should only take a few minutes, season to taste with salt and pepper, sprinkle over the parsley and transfer to a warm serving dish. Serve immediately with the rice and a green salad.

Goujons of sole with a lime mayonnaise & chips

SERVES 4–6 / PREP TIME: 20 MINUTES / COOKING TIME: ABOUT 1 HOUR

It's understandable that fish and chips are considered the national dish of Great Britain. We are an island after all, so fish is a big part of our heritage. Goujons of sole are really an upmarket version of the dish. I've put lime in the batter, which gives a little edge to the taste. Make it easy for yourself by doing the chips in the oven. It's heaven to stick them in the mayonnaise alongside the goujons.

6 large potatoes, preferably King Edward or Maris Piper, about 1.5kg in total, peeled and cut into chips
extra virgin olive oil
Maldon salt
4 medium eggs
juice of 2 small limes
250g plain flour
900g skinless lemon sole fillets, cut into strips
lime wedges

Mayonnaise
2 medium egg yolks, at room temperature
300ml peppery Tuscan extra virgin olive oil
grated zest and juice of 1 lime

Preheat the oven to 190°C/gas 5. Spread out the chips in one or two roasting tins, in one layer, and cover with olive oil. Add some salt. Roast for 40–60 minutes. When tender and golden brown, drain on kitchen paper and sprinkle with salt.

While the chips are cooking, make the mayonnaise. Put the egg yolks and a pinch of salt in a mixing bowl. Whisk the yolks together, then very slowly, drop by drop, add the olive oil while you are still whisking. It is important that you don't stop whisking. Keep adding the olive oil until the mayonnaise starts to form. When it has become the consistency you are happy with, stir in the lime zest and juice and season with salt to taste. Set aside in a cool place.

For the fish, beat the eggs in a mixing bowl. Squeeze in the lime juice and season with salt. Integrate all the ingredients. Put the flour in a separate bowl and season well with salt. Take each strip of sole and dip it into the egg, then turn it in the flour to coat well. Lay the coated fish on a board or plate, in one layer.

Liberally cover the bottom of a frying pan with olive oil. Heat the oil, then gently add the strips of fish without crowding them (cook them in batches if necessary). Fry until they are crispy and golden, turning when appropriate. Remove the fish and place them on kitchen paper to absorb any excess oil. Serve immediately with the mayonnaise, chips and lime wedges.

Lemon & fennel lacquered snapper

SERVES 4–6 / PREP TIME: 15 MINUTES / COOKING TIME: ABOUT 25 MINUTES

This great dish has a bit of a tongue-twister title – try saying it after you've had a glass or two of wine. When having friends over, I find it much easier to cook a whole fish than several individual portions and I think it looks better, too. Snapper is a delicious fish that is at home with most flavours. Serve this with steamed pak choy and garlic-roasted diced potatoes.

1 snapper or sea bass, about 1.5kg, scaled and cleaned
1 teaspoon fennel seeds
grated zest and juice of 2 lemons
1 tablespoon runny honey
2 garlic cloves, crushed
a bunch of fresh coriander
extra virgin olive oil
Maldon salt

Make sure you take the fish out of the fridge at least 30 minutes before cooking. This will help it to cook evenly.

Preheat the oven to 200°C/gas 6. Rinse the fish and pat dry, then place it in a roasting dish. Crush the fennel seeds in a mortar. In a bowl, combine the fennel seeds with the lemon zest and juice, honey and garlic. Stuff the cavity of the fish with half of the coriander. Pour over the lemon mixture, drizzle with a little olive oil and sprinkle with a pinch of salt.

Bake for about 25 minutes or until the flesh looks opaque and the skin will peel back easily from the flesh. Remove the fish to a hot serving dish. When serving, sprinkle each portion with coriander and the juices from the dish.

Another idea: Snapper with chermoula

Preheat the oven to 190°C/gas 5. Clean and scale a snapper or sea bass weighing about 1.5kg. Put 2 tablespoons of coriander seeds and 2 teaspoons of saffron threads in a small pan and dry roast until they smell fragrant. Don't let them brown. Pound the spices and a couple of generous pinches of salt in a mortar until fine. Add 2 cloves of garlic and continue pounding until you have a paste. Add 125ml extra virgin olive oil and a finely chopped bunch of fresh flat-leaf parsley, and combine well. Cut three slits on each side of the fish. Place the fish on a baking tray. Rub the spice paste all over the fish and in the cavity. Leave it to rest for at least 15 minutes, then bake for about 30 minutes or until cooked. Serve with couscous laden with fresh herbs, such as mint, parsley and basil, plus onions and pine nuts.

Fillets of brill on a bed of leeks, chanterelles & tarragon

SERVES 4–6 / PREP TIME: 10 MINUTES / COOKING TIME: 15 MINUTES

I love fish served on a bed of fresh, seasonal vegetables and herbs. It's a good way to keep the taste of the fish pure, while having a lovely amalgamation of flavours. Creamy mashed potatoes would be excellent with this. For wine, I'd recommend an Australian Semillon or a Gavi from Italy.

50g unsalted butter
6–8 thin leeks, trimmed
Maldon salt
250g chanterelles, washed and dried
a bunch of fresh tarragon, leaves only
freshly ground black pepper
extra virgin olive oil
4–6 brill fillets, about 400g each
plain flour for dusting

Melt the butter in a frying pan and add the leeks with a large pinch of salt. Cook on a moderate heat for a few minutes until tender. Toss in the mushrooms and let them soften; this will only take a couple of minutes. Stir in two-thirds of the tarragon leaves and season to taste with salt and pepper. Keep hot.

Lightly coat the bottom of another frying pan with olive oil and set on a moderate heat. Put a little flour in a mixing bowl and season well with salt and pepper. Dust the fillets of fish with the seasoned flour, then fry skin side down until golden brown. Turn the fillets over and cook for another minute.

Spoon the leek and chanterelle mixture on to hot serving plates and place the fish on top. Garnish with the remaining tarragon leaves and serve.

Coq au vin

SERVES 4–6 / PREP TIME: 10 MINUTES / COOKING TIME: 1¼ HOURS

I confess that until writing this book I'd never cooked this recipe. I couldn't get beyond the idea that it was popular in Sixties' bistros that had checked tablecloths and Mateus Rosé bottles with house-of-horror candle wax dripping down. But I've discovered that this is easy and delicious. If you don't have red wine use white, and relax if there's no brandy in the cupboard – just use some of the wine for deglazing.

8 teaspoons extra virgin olive oil
100g unsalted butter
1 medium chicken, about 1.5–2kg, jointed
plain flour for coating
Maldon salt
6 bacon rashers, diced
4 tablespoons brandy
1 bottle of Beaujolais
a fresh bouquet garni of thyme, parsley and bay leaf
225g baby onions, peeled
225g brown cap mushrooms, halved or quartered
a small bunch of fresh flat-leaf parsley, leaves only, finely chopped

Preheat the oven to 180°C/gas 4. Heat the olive oil and half the butter in a large flameproof casserole. Dip the chicken pieces into flour to coat reasonably well, then brown them in the butter and oil. Season well with salt. Remove with tongs.

Fry the bacon in the casserole. Add the brandy, turn up the heat and stir to deglaze the pan. Put back the chicken and cover with the Beaujolais. Add the bouquet garni. Bring to simmering point, then cover and place in the oven. Cook for about 1 hour or until the chicken is tender and the sauce has thickened.

Meanwhile, melt the remaining butter in a frying pan and sauté the onions until tender and golden. Add the mushrooms and fry until softened. About 10 minutes before the chicken has finished cooking, add the onions and mushrooms to the casserole. Scatter the chopped parsley over before serving.

Summer chicken casserole

SERVES 4–6 / PREP TIME: 20 MINUTES / COOKING TIME: 1 HOUR 20 MINUTES

If you have time the day before, slash the inside of the bird up into the breasts and stuff it with the onions and tarragon, then leave in the fridge for 24 hours so that the flavours from the tarragon and onion can really penetrate into the meat. Any summer vegetables will work well in this dish; I like the different colours of the green vegetables so I don't add carrots.

1 white or regular onion, roughly chopped
a bunch of fresh tarragon
1 medium chicken, about 1.5–2kg
extra virgin olive oil
10 garlic cloves, peeled
vegetable stock
16 small new potatoes, preferably Jersey Royals, scrubbed
10 baby onions, peeled
3 handfuls of fresh peas, shelled
2 handfuls of fresh broad beans, shelled
a handful of thin green beans, such as Kenyan beans

Stuff the chopped onion and tarragon into the body cavity of the chicken. Swirl olive oil over the bottom of a large flameproof casserole and heat over a high heat. Add the chicken with the garlic cloves and brown on both sides. Add enough stock to come halfway up the side of the chicken. Bring to the boil, then cover and simmer for 40 minutes.

Add the potatoes and baby onions. Cover again and cook for a further 15 minutes. Stir in the peas, broad beans and green beans and cook, covered, for 5 more minutes. Serve directly from the casserole dish at the table.

Autumn chicken & squash tagine with parsley & mint

SERVES 4–6 / PREP TIME: 20 MINUTES / COOKING TIME: 55 MINUTES

Tagines are Moroccan casseroles cooked in terracotta dishes. Autumn is a great time to make use of sweet potatoes and the different varieties of squash that have arrived at the greengrocers. They are all good for boosting your immune system for the winter. To go alongside, steam up some couscous and add flaked almonds, the teensiest bit of chilli and a little ground cinnamon.

extra virgin olive oil
1 chicken, about 2kg, cut into 8 pieces
3 large red onions, finely chopped
5 garlic cloves, crushed
2 cinnamon sticks
700g various kinds of squash, such as butternut, acorn and kabocha, peeled and cut into small cubes
700g sweet potatoes, peeled and cut into small cubes
600ml chicken or vegetable stock
Maldon salt
freshly ground black pepper
a small bunch of fresh flat-leaf parsley, finely chopped
a small bunch of fresh mint, leaves only, finely chopped

Coat the bottom of a large flameproof casserole with olive oil. When it is hot, add the chicken pieces, in batches if necessary, and brown them all over. Remove and keep warm.

Add the onions to the casserole and cook until soft, then add the garlic and cinnamon. Stir in the squash and sweet potatoes. Return the chicken to the pan and pour over the stock. Bring to the boil, then cover tightly and simmer for about 40 minutes or until the chicken is tender.

Season with salt and pepper and throw in the parsley and mint. Serve from the casserole dish, with couscous on the side.

Ossobuco

SERVES 4–6 / PREP TIME: 10 MINUTES / COOKING TIME: 1¾–2¼ HOURS

This classic Italian dish is customarily served with gremolata, which is a mixture of lemon zest, parsley and garlic, and risotto alla Milanese, a delicate saffron risotto. This ossobuco is cooked in 'bianco' – without tomato – which I think is more complementary to the gremolata and risotto.

plain flour for dusting
Maldon salt
4–6 thick slices of veal shin
2 tablespoons extra virgin olive oil
60g unsalted butter
2 red onions, finely chopped
2 garlic cloves, chopped
1 celery stick, finely chopped
½ bottle of dry white wine

Gremolata
2 teaspoons grated lemon zest
1 garlic clove, finely chopped
2 tablespoons finely chopped fresh flat-leaf parsley

Preheat the oven to 170°C/gas 3. Season some flour with salt and use to dust each piece of veal. Heat the olive oil in a large flameproof casserole on a high heat and brown the meat on both sides. Remove to a dish.

Add two-thirds of the butter to the casserole and gently sauté the onions, garlic and celery. Season with a little salt. When the vegetables are soft return the meat and its juices to the pan. Pour over the wine. Bring to simmering point and reduce the liquid by half. Then cover and place in the oven. Cook for 1½–2 hours or until the meat is falling off the bone. Turn the meat halfway through the cooking.

Remove the meat to a serving dish. Set the casserole on top of the cooker and reduce the sauce a little further to thicken. Add the remaining butter, then spoon over the veal.

Mix together the ingredients for the gremolata and sprinkle over each piece of veal. Serve immediately with risotto.

Casserole of pheasant with thyme, apples & cider

SERVES 4-6 / PREP TIME: 15 MINUTES / COOKING TIME: 1¼ HOURS

Casseroles are hearty and warming and, with the aromatic union of different vegetables and herbs, they make a lovely greeting from a cold, brisk walk before lunch. Use hen pheasants instead of cocks as the meat is more tender. I'll find any excuse to have a glass of cider and this naturally calls for one.

Maldon salt
2 large hen pheasants
a bunch of fresh thyme
6 tablespoons extra virgin olive oil
100g unsalted butter
14 shallots, peeled
3 garlic cloves, crushed
7 Cox's apples, quartered and cored
2 teaspoons apple jelly or redcurrant jelly
400ml cider
vegetable or chicken stock (optional)
300ml double cream

Preheat the oven to 180°C/gas 4. Salt the pheasants, then stuff them with two-thirds of the thyme. Heat the olive oil and butter in a large flameproof casserole and fry the birds until they are golden brown all over. Remove them, then fry the shallots and garlic until soft. Put the pheasants back in the casserole, pushing the shallots up and over the top of the birds so they don't sit on the bottom. Add the quartered apples, apple jelly and the rest of the thyme (keep a couple of sprigs for the garnish). Pour over the cider. If you feel you need more liquid, top up with vegetable or chicken stock. Add a large pinch of salt to the liquid. Cover the casserole and place in the oven. Cook for about 40 minutes, checking occasionally and giving it a bit of a stir.

Pour in the cream, then return to the oven, uncovered, and cook for a further 10–15 minutes. Check for seasoning. Sprinkle the reserved thyme leaves on top and serve from the casserole dish.

Chicken scaloppine

SERVES 4–6 / PREP TIME: 15 MINUTES / COOKING TIME: 10 MINUTES

This classic Italian dish has been part of my repertoire for years. Use good ingredients for this – organic chicken, buffalo mozzarella and fresh olives as opposed to canned – because it will make a big difference. This might become your own 'signature' dish. Serve it with a wild rocket salad and crispy sliced potatoes fried in olive oil with chilli flakes.

extra virgin olive oil
2 onions, finely chopped
2 garlic cloves, finely chopped
2 tablespoons tomato purée
2 x 400g cans chopped tomatoes
2 teaspoons caster sugar
125g small black olives
a bunch of fresh basil, leaves only
Maldon salt
freshly ground black pepper
3 large chicken breast fillets
plain flour for dusting
6 thin slices of prosciutto
6 thin slices of buffalo mozzarella

Coat the bottom of a saucepan with olive oil. When hot, add the onions and garlic and cook over a moderate heat until soft. Stir in the tomato purée, then the tomatoes, sugar, olives and basil leaves (keep six leaves for the garnish). Season with salt and pepper and bring to a gentle simmer. Leave to cook while preparing the chicken.

Slice horizontally into the chicken breasts to split them in half, then use a rolling pin to pound the smooth side of each piece of chicken to flatten it. Dust the chicken scaloppine with flour. Heat some olive oil in a frying pan and cook the scaloppine for 3–4 minutes on each side.

Preheat the grill to high. Put the tomato sauce in a large flameproof dish or roasting tin and lay the scaloppine evenly on top. Put a folded-over slice of prosciutto on each scaloppine, then a slice of mozzarella and then a basil leaf. Place under the grill until the mozzarella starts to melt and become golden. Garnish with fresh basil and serve immediately.

Warm crispy duck with mint & pine nuts in an orange dressing

SERVES 4 / PREP TIME: 10 MINUTES / COOKING TIME: 15–20 MINUTES

The crispy golden fat on a 'magret', which is the meaty breast from a Barbary or Muscovy duck, is hard to beat. And when the duck is tossed in a salad there is a delicious contrast between the cold fresh ingredients and the warmth of the meat. The lovely thing about this salad is that the orange and mint balance the richness of the duck beautifully. I like to add a little bit of rocket to the salad, as the bitter leaves combine so well with the sweet orange. If you prefer, use unsalted cashew nuts rather than pine nuts – they work extremely well, too.

2–4 magrets (large duck breasts)
Maldon salt
juice of 2 oranges
4 teaspoons extra virgin olive oil
4 teaspoons white wine vinegar
freshly ground black pepper
a handful of fresh mint leaves, finely chopped
a bunch of rocket
a handful of pine nuts

Preheat the grill to high. Score the skin and fat on the duck breasts without cutting into the meat, then salt well. Place under the grill and cook for 15–20 minutes, turning when appropriate.

Meanwhile, in a jam jar, combine the orange juice, olive oil, vinegar, a pinch of salt and a good grinding of pepper. Shake well.

When the duck is ready, cut it into thin slices and place in a serving bowl. Add the mint, rocket and pine nuts and pour over the dressing. Mix well and serve immediately.

Fillet of venison stuffed with cranberries, juniper & rosemary

SERVES 4–6 / PREP TIME: 15 MINUTES / COOKING TIME: 30 MINUTES

This is a wonderfully festive dish and the jolliness of the tart cranberries, rosemary and juniper give it a warming, fragrant pungency. I serve it with potatoes roasted in goose fat – before cooking I slash them and insert a bay leaf. Most butchers should supply you with goose fat, or you can find it in larger supermarkets.

extra virgin olive oil
2 shallots, finely chopped
1 garlic clove, finely chopped
2 tablespoons fresh or frozen cranberries
1 teaspoon juniper berries, crushed
1 heaped teaspoon caster sugar
2 teaspoons finely chopped fresh rosemary
1 venison fillet, about 1.5kg
Maldon salt
a glass of full-bodied red wine
1 heaped teaspoon redcurrant jelly

Preheat the oven to 220°C/gas 7. Drizzle olive oil over the bottom of a saucepan and heat, then gently sauté the shallots and garlic. Add the cranberries, juniper berries, sugar and rosemary and cook gently until the cranberries are soft. Remove from the heat.

Slit the fillet lengthways in half, without cutting all the way through. Open it up like a book. Spoon the cranberry mixture evenly on top, then reshape the fillet and tie up with string. (If you prefer, you can cut it across to make six individual pieces.) Place in a roasting tin and drizzle with olive oil and salt.

Set the tin on top of the cooker and sear the fillet on all sides. Pour half of the red wine around the meat, then transfer to the oven and roast for 25 minutes.

Remove the fillet to a hot serving platter. Set the tin on top of the cooker, add the rest of the red wine and stir to deglaze the juices. Add the redcurrant jelly and reduce until thickened and syrupy. Serve with the sliced venison.

Leg of lamb with fresh spring herbs & shallots

SERVES 4–6 / PREP TIME: 20 MINUTES / COOKING TIME: 1 HOUR 20 MINUTES

Lamb is a meat I associate with the spring, just when there are a zillion fresh herbs waiting to deliver the most sublime flavours. Put me anywhere that herbs are growing and I start to salivate at the thought of all those different flavours ready to take me on a culinary journey. In this recipe the shallots become all melty and caramelised, making the most sumptuous gravy for the lamb. Rosemary roast potatoes will be happy to go along for the ride, or garlic mash is equally delicious. For veggies, cook spinach leaves until wilted with a squeeze of lemon, a drizzle of olive oil, and some salt and pepper.

1 leg of lamb on the bone, about 2kg
a few fresh rosemary leaves, finely chopped
a few fresh thyme leaves, finely chopped
a few fresh sage leaves, finely chopped
a few fresh chives, finely chopped
1 teaspoon runny honey
3 new season garlic cloves, finely chopped
Maldon salt
extra virgin olive oil
12 shallots, peeled

Preheat the oven to 230°C/gas 8. Take the lamb out of the fridge and leave it at room temperature for about 15 minutes. Meanwhile, keep a few of the chopped herbs for the garnish and mix the remaining herbs together with the honey, garlic, a large pinch of salt and 2 teaspoons of olive oil.

Take a sharp knife and make an incision into the meat underneath the skin at the opposite end from the bone. Go in fairly deep to make a pocket between the skin and the meat. Stuff in the herb mixture as far as you can, then pat the skin down on top. Put the lamb in a roasting tin and add the shallots. Pour a generous amount of olive oil over the meat and shallots and sprinkle salt over the meat. Roast for 20 minutes, then turn the heat down to 200°C/gas 6. Baste the meat with the juices in the tin, then roast for a further 15 minutes per 500g (for medium rare) – this will be about 1 hour more for a 2kg joint.

Remove the lamb to a carving board and leave to rest for 10 minutes. Lift 10 of the shallots out of the tin and keep hot. Squash down the remaining two shallots in the tin to mix them into the juices and scrape any sticky bits off the bottom. Put the tin on top of the cooker and turn up the heat to high. Bring to the boil and let the gravy reduce a little. Garnish the lamb with the reserved herbs, then carve and serve with the gravy and whole shallots.

Shoulder of lamb with 20 cloves of garlic

SERVES 4–6 / PREP TIME: 30 MINUTES / COOKING TIME: 2¾–3¼ HOURS

I like lamb on the pink side but also love it when it has cooked for hours and the meat is falling off the bone. If you fancy having more vegetables in this casserole, throw in a few leeks 10 minutes before the end of the cooking. Some finely chopped fresh parsley over the top will make the juices even more savoury.

1 shoulder of lamb, about 1.6kg, excess fat trimmed off
extra virgin olive oil
20 garlic cloves, peeled
300ml dry white wine
100ml water
a sprig of fresh thyme
2 sprigs of fresh rosemary
Maldon salt
2 teaspoons redcurrant jelly

Preheat the oven to 220°C/gas 7. Lightly pierce the lamb all over with the sharp tip of a knife. Drizzle olive oil over the bottom of a large flameproof casserole. When the oil is hot, brown the fat side of the lamb. Turn the lamb over and add the garlic cloves. Pour in the wine and water. Add the thyme and rosemary and sprinkle the lamb generously with salt. Add the redcurrant jelly. Bring the liquid to the boil, then transfer the casserole to the oven. Cook for 30 minutes.

Reduce the heat to 150°C/gas 2. Cover the casserole and cook for a further 2–2½ hours or until the meat comes easily from the bone. Serve with mashed potatoes and sliced carrots cooked in butter with thyme leaves (cook, without any water, in a covered pan on top of the cooker for about 15 minutes).

Another idea: Braised peas with lettuce & spring onions

This summer vegetable dish is a delicious accompaniment to lamb. Melt 50g unsalted butter in a medium saucepan and add 6 chopped spring onions, 6 Little Gem lettuce leaves and 450g fresh peas. Stir to coat with the butter, then add 3 tablespoons of water followed by a pinch of caster sugar and two generous pinches of salt. Gently bring to simmering point, then cover and cook on a very low heat for 15–20 minutes, giving the pan a shake now and then. Add some more water if necessary. Check the seasoning, scatter over a few roughly chopped mint leaves and serve.

Boneless shoulder of lamb with herb stuffing & sauteed leeks, black olives & thyme

SERVES 4–6 / PREP TIME: 20 MINUTES / COOKING TIME: 1 HOUR 5 MINUTES

This is a useful way of cooking lamb when you want to put in a flavourful stuffing. The fresh rosemary and spring onions give the meat a great punch. I never can resist mashed potatoes and with this lamb I suggest you mash in a few garlic cloves, adding them to the potatoes while they are cooking.

1 boned shoulder of lamb, about 1.5kg
a few fresh rosemary leaves, finely chopped
4 teaspoons fresh breadcrumbs
3 spring onions, finely chopped
2 garlic cloves, crushed
1 heaped teaspoon redcurrant jelly
extra virgin olive oil
Maldon salt

Sautéed leeks
25g unsalted butter
4 teaspoons extra virgin olive oil
9 thin leeks, sliced
3 sprigs of fresh thyme, leaves only
10 pitted black Provençal olives, chopped
freshly ground black pepper

Preheat the oven to 230°C/gas 8. Take the lamb out of the fridge and leave at room temperature for about 15 minutes. Meanwhile, mix together the rosemary, breadcrumbs, spring onions, garlic, redcurrant jelly and 4 teaspoons olive oil. Add a pinch of salt.

Spoon the rosemary mixture on to the centre of the meat and roll it over to enclose. Secure it with string and put it in a roasting tin. Drizzle over some olive oil and sprinkle liberally with salt. Roast for 20 minutes, then turn down the heat to 200°C/gas 6. Roast for a further 15 minutes per 500g if you like lamb medium rare – this will be about 45 minutes more for a 1.5kg joint.

Meanwhile, melt the butter in a saucepan and add the olive oil and then add the leeks. Stir in the thyme leaves and olives. Sauté gently until the leeks are soft. Season to taste with salt and pepper and keep warm.

Serve the lamb with all the juices from the tin and the sautéed leeks.

Seared fillet of beef with roast vegetables & basil

SERVES 4–6 / PREP TIME: 30 MINUTES / COOKING TIME: 45 MINUTES

The combination of vegetables here gives a gorgeous rainbow of hues. The yellow of the sweetcorn, the fuchsia beetroot, the scarlet peppers and the emerald basil will set your hunger pangs in motion. Build the vegetables high on a plate to give a little architecture to the dish and a feeling of abundance to your guests. I recommend buying really good Scotch pedigree beef such as Aberdeen Angus.

1.5kg piece of fillet of beef, trimmed
Maldon salt
extra virgin olive oil
Dijon mustard, to serve

Vegetables

1 small red pepper, deseeded and cut into squares
1 small yellow pepper, deseeded and cut into squares
1 large red onion, roughly chopped
2 courgettes, roughly chopped
2 beetroots, sliced and each slice quartered
2 large garlic cloves, crushed
450g vine-ripened cherry tomatoes, skinned
50g pitted black Provençal olives, chopped
4 tablespoons extra virgin olive oil
Maldon salt
1 corn on the cob, leaves and silky threads removed
freshly ground black pepper
a small bunch of fresh basil, leaves only

Preheat the oven to 240°C/gas 9. Arrange the peppers, onion, courgettes, beetroots, garlic, tomatoes and olives in a roasting tin. Drizzle with the olive oil and salt and toss everything around to get a good coating. Place the tin on the highest shelf in the oven and roast for 30–40 minutes or until all the vegetables are cooked but still retain a crunch.

Meanwhile, cook the sweetcorn in a pan of boiling water for 4–5 minutes or until tender. Remove from the heat and drain. When cool enough to handle, shave the kernels off the cob. Set aside.

When the vegetables are roasted, transfer them to a flat serving platter and pile the sweetcorn on top. Season with freshly ground black pepper and scatter the basil leaves over. Keep warm.

Preheat a ridged cast-iron grill pan. Cut the beef fillet into 1cm thick slices. With a rolling pin give them a healthy bash on both sides. Season them with salt and brush with olive oil on both sides. When the grill pan is hot, char-grill the slices of beef for about 1 minute on each side (do this in batches if necessary and keep warm in a low oven). Serve immediately with the roast vegetables and Dijon mustard.

Pork fillet with caramelised grapefruit & fennel seeds

SERVES 4 / PREP TIME: 10 MINUTES / COOKING TIME: 25-30 MINUTES

Citrus zest gives a delightful zip without the sharpness of the juice, as it's the oil from the skin that comes through. For this dish you can use whatever citrus fruit you have lying about, whether it's tangerines, oranges, lemons or lime – the more the merrier. The caramelised grapefruit gives a dynamic sweet and sour quality. I suggest some fried or roast potatoes with fresh rosemary or thyme to accompany this and some steamed winter greens.

2 pink grapefruits
1 or 2 pork fillets (tenderloin), about 450g in total
1 teaspoon fennel seeds
grated zest of 1/2 lemon
grated zest of 1/2 lime
2 teaspoons soft brown sugar
a few fresh thyme leaves
extra virgin olive oil
Maldon salt

Preheat the oven to 190°C/gas 5. Grate the zest from the grapefruit, then peel the fruit and separate the segments. Lay the pork fillet in a roasting dish. Make eight incisions along the top of the meat and stuff with the fennel seeds. In a bowl, mix the grapefruit zest and segments with the lemon and lime zests, brown sugar and thyme. Add to the roasting dish. Drizzle all with olive oil and season with salt.

Cover with foil, place in the oven and roast for 25–30 minutes or until the pork is cooked through. Halfway through the roasting time, baste the pork with the juices in the dish, and 10 minutes before the end of the cooking remove the foil. Cut the pork into discs and serve with the grapefruit and juices from the roasting dish.

Vietnamese roast pork

SERVES 4–6 / PREP TIME: 10 MINUTES PLUS 1 HOUR TO OVERNIGHT MARINATING

COOKING TIME: 1½ HOURS

Peel some Cox's apples and stew them until they are mushy, then throw in some chopped fresh coriander leaves, and serve alongside the pork with some crispy, golden roast potatoes. A bottle of chilled Sancerre will complement the pork more than adequately.

1 boned and rolled loin of pork, about 1.5kg (ask your butcher to score the fat)
250ml soy sauce
2 tablespoons white wine vinegar
1 heaped tablespoon soft brown sugar
a bunch of spring onions, green part only

Place the pork in a deep narrow dish – there should be a clear space of about 2cm on each side of the meat. Pour over the soy sauce and add the vinegar and sugar. The meat should almost be covered with liquid. Leave for at least 1 hour or overnight if possible.

Preheat the oven to its highest setting. Remove the meat from the marinade (reserve the marinade) and put it in a roasting tin. Spoon about 1cm of marinade over and around the pork. Place in the middle of the oven and roast for 30 minutes. Keep adding more marinade as it bubbles and evaporates. Turn down the heat to 180°C/gas 4 and roast for a further 1 hour or until the fat has crackled and becomes crispy and golden.

With scissors, snip the green part of the spring onions over the meat and serve it with apple sauce and potatoes.

Another idea: Texan-style pork ribs

In a large bowl, combine 3 crushed cloves of garlic, 4 teaspoons of tomato purée, 2 tablespoons of soft brown sugar, 4 teaspoons of Worcestershire sauce, 4 teaspoons of tomato ketchup, 4 teaspoons of white wine vinegar, 1 teaspoon of Tabasco sauce, 2 large pinches of pimentón (sweet smoked paprika) and 2 pinches of Maldon salt. Coat 1.5kg pork ribs (in one piece, cut in half) with the paste, then leave to marinate for as long as you can.

Preheat the oven to 200°C/gas 6. Place the ribs on a rack over a roasting tin. Bake for 35–40 minutes or until they are cooked. Serve with baked potatoes topped with crème fraîche, a sprinkle of chives and a pinch of paprika.

Roast chicken stuffed with lemon thyme served with lemon & parsley mashed potatoes

SERVES 4–6 / PREP TIME: 30 MINUTES / COOKING TIME: 1 HOUR 40 MINUTES

Roast chicken is both delicious and easy – what I like to call low-maintenance cooking. There's half an hour between each basting, which means you can have a bath or read the paper. There's also time to do something special with the accompanying vegetables. Mashed potatoes are always good with chicken, and this recipe adds a little dynamism with the lemon zest and parsley. Be sure you take the chicken out of the fridge at least 30 minutes before cooking.

1 medium chicken, about 1.2–2kg
a large bunch of fresh lemon thyme
1 red onion, cut into wedges
1 garlic bulb
extra virgin olive oil
Maldon salt

Mashed potatoes
12–18 medium potatoes, such as King Edward or Desiree, peeled and cut into even pieces
a large knob of unsalted butter
full fat milk
freshly ground black pepper
grated zest of 1 lemon
a small handful of flat-leaf parsley leaves, roughly chopped

Preheat the oven to 200°C/gas 6. Place the chicken in a roasting dish. Crush the lemon thyme in your fist, then rub it all over the bird. Stuff the thyme into the body cavity with half of the onion. Put the garlic bulb and remaining onion in the dish alongside the chicken. Pour olive oil boldly over the bird, then sprinkle with salt, which should sit on the skin almost like a crust.

Put the dish into the oven and roast for about 1 hour and 20 minutes, basting every 30 minutes or so with the juices in the dish. To check if the bird is done, gently insert a knife or skewer between the leg and the breast; the juices should run out clear.

Remove from the oven, tipping the chicken so the juices run out of the body cavity into the dish. Put the chicken on a plate and set aside in a warm place to rest for at least 20 minutes. Set aside the roasting dish with the juices, garlic bulb and onion wedges.

About 10 minutes before the chicken is cooked, make the mashed potatoes. Put the potatoes in a large saucepan with plenty of cold, generously salted water. Bring to the boil, then cook for about 20 minutes or until a fork easily penetrates the potatoes. Drain well. Return the potatoes to the pan, add the

butter and start mashing. When you've mashed out the lumps, slowly add the milk, adding enough to make the texture you like. Add a large pinch of salt and a few big turns of the pepper grinder. Fold in the lemon zest and parsley. Keep hot.

Break up the garlic bulb, take half of the cloves and squeeze the cooked garlic out of the skins into the juices in the roasting dish (keep the rest of the garlic cloves and the onion wedges for people who want to eat them). Reheat the juices in the roasting dish on top of the cooker, mashing in the garlic. Serve the chicken with the mashed potatoes and the garlicky juices.

Chicken satay with peanut sauce

SERVES 4–6 / PREP TIME: 25 MINUTES PLUS AT LEAST 4 HOURS MARINATING

COOKING TIME: 25 MINUTES

Although this dish is a little labour-intensive, it is worth the time. It's perfect for kids, and if the weather is fine you can cook the satay on the barbecue. The peanut sauce can be made ahead of time and then reheated gently. Most of the ingredients can be found in larger supermarkets, and all Asian supermarkets will stock them. Freshly ground peanut butter is available in most healthfood shops.

2 garlic cloves, finely chopped
1 tablespoon chilli oil
4 tablespoons vegetable oil
2 teaspoons toasted sesame oil
2 tablespoons sweet soy sauce
Maldon salt
freshly ground black pepper
2 large chicken breast fillets, cut into 1 cm cubes

Peanut sauce
2 large fresh red chillies, deseeded and chopped
3 garlic cloves, crushed
1 teaspoon dried shrimp paste
2 tablespoons groundnut oil
2 kaffir lime leaves, torn
400ml coconut milk
250g peanut butter, freshly ground (without added, oil, salt and sugar)
1 tablespoon palm sugar
juice of 2 limes or 1 lemon, plus wedges to serve
Maldon salt

In a large bowl, combine the garlic, oils, soy sauce and some salt and pepper. Stir well to integrate all of the ingredients. Add the chicken, mixing well into the marinade. Cover and refrigerate for at least 4 hours.

For the sauce, pound the chillies and garlic with the shrimp paste in a mortar. Heat the groundnut oil in a heavy-based saucepan and fry the chilli mixture over a low heat for a few minutes. Mix in the lime leaves, then add the coconut milk. Stir well and bring to a simmer. Remove from the heat and mix in the peanut butter and palm sugar until well combined. Return the pan to the heat and simmer the sauce until it has a creamy consistency. Stir in the lime or lemon juice and add salt to taste. If necessary add warm water to thin the sauce. Set aside and keep warm.

Preheat the barbecue or grill. Thread the chicken pieces on to 20 wooden satay skewers that have been soaked in water. Barbecue or grill the skewers for about 10 minutes or until the chicken is cooked, regularly turning and basting the chicken with the marinade. Serve with the warm peanut sauce for dipping, a lime or lemon wedge and some steamed Thai fragrant rice.

seven
sweet things – puddings, tarts, pies and cakes

Summer pudding

SERVES 4-6 / PREP TIME: 20 MINUTES PLUS OVERNIGHT CHILLING

Summer pudding has to go down as one of the simplest yet most inspired puddings – in my mind it definitely ranks in the top ten of great puddings. Lashings, and I mean that in the Enid Blyton sense, of thick ivory-coloured cream are needed to blanket the fuchsia delight. A quick tip for removing redcurrants and white currants from their stalks is to take a fork and gently slip the stalk through the tines.

500g raspberries
175g redcurrants, removed from stalks
50g white currants, removed from stalks
110g blackcurrants, removed from stalks
160g caster sugar
8–10 medium-sliced white bread, crusts removed
a few fresh mint leaves for decoration
double cream, to serve

Put the fruit and sugar in a large heavy-based saucepan over a moderate heat. Let it cook for a few minutes, just until the sugar has dissolved and the juices from the fruit begin to run. Do not overcook. Remove from the heat.

Line an 850ml pudding basin with slices of bread, overlapping them so that there are no gaps. Pour in the fruit, holding back one-third of the juice in reserve. Seal the fruit in the basin with the final pieces of bread. Place a saucer or plate on top and weight it. Leave in the fridge overnight.

When ready to serve, turn the pudding out of the basin into a serving dish. Use the reserved juice to cover up any white patches on the bread. Decorate with mint leaves and serve immediately, with double cream.

Caramelised apricots & nectarines with vanilla mascarpone

SERVES 4–6 / PREP TIME: 15 MINUTES / COOKING TIME: 20 MINUTES

One very simple and delicious way of eating apricots and nectarines is to roast them with a little sugar and then eat them with vanilla-flavoured mascarpone. It doesn't have to be mascarpone – you can use thick double cream instead, with some soft brown sugar on top if you prefer it to be a little sweeter. I tend to go for organic fruit if I can, especially if the skin is to be eaten. If the nectarines are hard to cut neatly in half, just cut them from the stone in elegant even slices.

12 apricots, cut in half and stoned
6 nectarines, cut in half and stoned
caster sugar
100g unsalted butter
450g mascarpone
2 vanilla pods, split lengthways
a few fresh mint leaves for decoration

Preheat the oven to 200°C/gas 6. Have two roasting dishes at the ready. Put the halved apricots in one dish and the nectarines in the other. Sprinkle the fruit with sugar – about 2 teaspoons for each dish – and dot with butter. Place in the oven and roast for 20 minutes.

Meanwhile, put the mascarpone in a bowl. Use the tip of a teaspoon to scoop up the tiny black seeds from the vanilla pods. Add them to the mascarpone and mix them in well. Decorate the apricots and nectarines with fresh mint leaves and serve with the mascarpone.

Another idea: Toffee apples with cinnamon crème fraîche

You can prepare other fruit, such as banana or pineapple, in the same way, but apple works the best. Peel, core and cut into eighths 6 Granny Smith apples. Put them in a mixing bowl and toss with 4 tablespoons of caster sugar, 1½ teaspoons of ground cinnamon and 3 tablespoons of water. Set a heavy-based frying pan on a moderate heat and add the apples. Let them start to caramelise and turn golden, then turn them over. Remove when they are caramelised on both sides. Place 250g crème fraîche in a little serving bowl and sprinkle with ½ teaspoon of ground cinnamon. Serve with the hot apples.

Charles I Christmas orange jelly

SERVES 4–6 / PREP TIME: 20 MINUTES PLUS ABOUT 2 HOURS CHILLING

Originally oranges were found in Burma, or Myanmar, as it is also known. They were taken to the Holy Lands and were introduced by the Moors into Spain in the 11th century. Around the time of Charles I, orange jelly was very popular in England at Christmas. It makes a change from Christmas pud, or a rather delicious addition to it.

8 large oranges
1 tablespoon Marsala
75g caster sugar
2 leaves of gelatine

Orange cream
225ml thick double cream
grated zest of 1/2 orange
2 teaspoons Marsala

Take the zest from two of the oranges and put it to soak in the Marsala. Cut the rest of the oranges in half and gently squeeze out the juice so that you can use the cases for the orange jelly. Carefully remove the rest of the pulp and discard. Measure the orange juice and make it up to 600ml with extra juice from the other cranges if necessary. Put it in a saucepan with the sugar and bring to the boil, stirring well to make sure the sugar has dissolved. Remove from the heat.

Soak the gelatine leaves in a bowl of cold water for 10 minutes, then squeeze out the excess water. Stir the gelatine into the warm orange juice mixture together with the Marsala and orange zest. Pour gently into the empty orange cases and chill for 2 hours or until set. Serve with thick double cream laced with grated orange zest and Marsala.

Pimm's jelly

SERVES 4–6 / PREP TIME: 25 MINUTES PLUS 3 HOURS CHILLING

Pimm's has to be one of the best summer drinks there is, with plenty of luscious fruit loaded with sweet alcohol and laced with mint. This is just another way of enjoying it, with the added attraction of it being encased in sweet fruity jelly.

6 leaves of gelatine
1 litre fizzy lemonade, preferably Whites
50g caster sugar
300ml Pimm's (either gin cup or vodka cup)
4 oranges, peeled, thinly sliced and the slices quartered
1 apple, quartered, cored and thinly sliced
1/4 cucumber, diced
20 fresh mint leaves
single or double cream, to serve (optional)

Soak the gelatine leaves in a bowl of cold water for 10 minutes, then squeeze out the excess water. Put the lemonade and sugar in a saucepan and heat gently until the sugar has dissolved. Remove from the heat and stir in the gelatine until completely melted. When cool, mix in the Pimm's.

In a large glass serving dish, combine half the oranges, apple, cucumber and mint with half the Pimm's mixture. Chill for 1 1/2 hours to set the jelly. Keep the remaining Pimm's mixture liquid at room temperature.

Pour on the remaining Pimm's mixture and add the rest of the fruit. Chill for another 1 1/2 hours or until completely set. Serve with or without cream.

Honey-roasted oranges with rosemary cream

SERVES 4-6 / PREP TIME: 15 MINUTES / COOKING TIME: ABOUT 1 HOUR

So often we see the display of beautiful oranges sitting on the grocery shelves and think we must have them – it will be fresh orange juice for breakfast, or a healthy snack. Then somehow freshly squeezed juice only seems to fit into the Sunday morning agenda, and that's when you don't have a hangover. It's also easier to open a pack of biscuits than peel an orange, so more often than not they are left in the fruit basket. This is an easy dessert to make and ensures that the oranges won't be wasted. I love putting fruits and herbs together, and rosemary works really well with oranges. It's unexpected but so compatible.

8 oranges
a few fresh rosemary leaves
150ml orange flower honey
225ml double cream

Preheat the oven to 180°C/gas 4. Grate the zest from two of the oranges; peel and thickly slice the remaining oranges.

Place the orange slices in a large ovenproof dish. Keep aside a pinch of the orange zest and a little rosemary, and add the rest to the orange slices. Drizzle over the honey. Roast for just over 1 hour or until the oranges are dark and caramelised.

Whip the cream until it will form soft peaks. Finely chop the remaining rosemary and stir it into the whipped cream along with the reserved orange zest. Serve with the roast oranges.

Another idea: Roasted pineapple with mint sugar

Preheat the oven to 220°C/gas 7. Trim the skin off 2 large pineapples, then cut into either rings or segments. Place the pineapple in an ovenproof dish and roast for about 20 minutes or until it has released its juices and is browning slightly. Meanwhile, put 100g icing sugar and a bunch of fresh mint leaves in a blender and blend until finely chopped.

Place the hot pineapple in a serving dish and sprinkle with the grated zest of 1 lime and the mint sugar. Serve with vanilla ice cream.

Stewed plums with Italian almond rice pudding

SERVES 4–6 / PREP TIME: 10 MINUTES PLUS COOLING / COOKING TIME: 30–35 MINUTES

At the end of summer, plums are plentiful and are delicious stewed with a little sugar and vanilla. They work wonders with a creamy Italian rice pudding, which soaks up their sweet rich juices beautifully. The pudding is made with Arborio rice, which gives a lovely sticky feeling to the pudding. I like to use a variety of Italian plums called Fortune, as their dark cerise colour makes a lovely visual contrast to the milky rice pudding. Biscotti, which are the hard, sweet Italian biscuits, are an added attraction if you feel you need a crunchy counterpart.

8 red plums
55g caster sugar
1 vanilla pod, split lengthways
2 tablespoons water
icing sugar, sifted

Rice pudding
225g Arborio or other risotto rice
1.2 litres full fat milk
2 teaspoons finely grated lemon zest
100g caster sugar
50g whole blanched almonds, coarsely chopped
1 teaspoon vanilla extract
icing sugar, sifted, for decoration

Put the plums, sugar, vanilla pod and water into a saucepan. Cover and cook for 10–15 minutes or until the plums are soft but not mushy. Remove them from the heat and leave to cool to room temperature.

For the rice pudding, combine the rice, milk, lemon zest, sugar, almonds and vanilla extract in a heavy-based saucepan. Cook over a moderate heat, stirring occasionally, for about 20 minutes or until most of the milk has been absorbed by the rice.

Sprinkle the plums with a little sifted icing sugar and serve with the warm rice pudding.

Blackberry & apple pie

SERVES 4–6 / PREP TIME: 25 MINUTES PLUS 30 MINUTES CHILLING

COOKING TIME: ABOUT 40 MINUTES

Succulent, shiny black clusters of beads, full of sweet cerise juice, mixed with sugary tart apples and crusty buttery pastry, served with lashings of Jersey double cream. Do I need to say more?

6 Granny Smith apples, peeled, quartered and cored
200g blackberries
4 tablespoons caster sugar
single or double cream, to serve

Pastry
350g plain flour, plus extra for dusting
2 teaspoons caster sugar
200g cold, unsalted butter, cut into chunks
about 3 tablespoons ice cold water
4 teaspoons milk

To make the pastry, put the flour, sugar and butter in a mixing bowl and combine with the tips of your fingers until the mixture resembles breadcrumbs. Slowly add the water and squidge away until you have a dough. Roll this into a smooth ball. Cover with cling film or a tea towel and chill for about 30 minutes.

Preheat the oven to 200°C/gas 6. Chuck the apple quarters, blackberries and caster sugar into a large round or oval pie dish. Roll out the pastry on a floured board and use it to cover the dish. Flatten down the edges with a fork and cut away any excess pastry. Make two small incisions in the middle of the pastry. Brush all over with milk and decorate with any surplus pastry.

Pop in the oven and bake for about 40 minutes or until the pastry is crisp and golden. Let it cool for a few minutes, then serve with cream.

Another idea: Summer cherry berry pie

Use 700g of cherries, raspberries, blueberries, blackberries and redcurrants. Preheat the oven to 200°C/gas 6. On a floured surface, roll out 750g of puff pastry to create a 30cm round. Place on a baking tray greased with butter. Pile most of the fruit in the middle. Beat an egg with a little water, then brush over the edge of the pastry. Bring the pastry edge into the centre, pleating and folding it over the fruit. Leave a gap in the middle and fill with a few berries (keep some back for decoration). Brush the pastry with the egg wash and sprinkle with caster sugar. Bake for 30 minutes. If the pastry starts to brown too much, cover loosely with foil. Dust with icing sugar and serve with the remaining fruit and clotted cream.

Baked passion fruit crunch

SERVES 4–6 / PREP TIME: 20 MINUTES / COOKING TIME: 25 MINUTES

Passion fruit is a delightful little tropical fruit that lends itself with great ardour to all things sweet due to its slightly edgy sour taste. It has a very concentrated flavour so it can be used more sparingly than other fruit. It's ripe when the egg-shaped, dark purple shell is slightly wrinkled. Buy a couple of extra ones and eat them out of the shell with a spoon.

125g unsalted butter
100g plain digestive biscuits, crushed
150g cream cheese
150g ricotta cheese
240ml double cream
142ml soured cream
100g caster sugar
3 medium eggs
9 passion fruits, halved

Preheat the oven to 170°C/gas 3. Melt the butter in a saucepan, then add the biscuits and stir until they absorb the butter. Spoon into a 20cm flan dish and flatten the biscuits to form a base.

In a mixing bowl, combine the cream cheese, ricotta, double cream, soured cream and sugar. Beat with an electric mixer until all the ingredients are well integrated. Add the eggs, mixing in well. Stir in the pulp from the passion fruits. Pour over the biscuit base. Bake for about 25 minutes or until the top is golden and the filling has set. Leave to cool, then chill until ready to eat.

Quince & honey crumble

SERVES 4–6 / PREP TIME: 25 MINUTES / COOKING TIME: 35 MINUTES

This pudding always makes me think of The Owl and the Pussy Cat, who ate quince with a runcible spoon – whatever that may be. Quince is a beautiful fruit, with a soft yellow exterior covered in a soft, pale grey down. When heated it produces the prettiest deep pink flesh. If you place a quince in a cupboard it will give off a delicious aroma. I even put them in my clothes cupboard. Quinces don't rot; they just wilt after a month or two.

3 quinces, peeled, cored and sliced
400ml water
4 teaspoons caster sugar
4 pears, peeled, cored and sliced
1 vanilla pod, split lengthways
2 teaspoons runny honey
grated zest of 1 lemon
a knob of unsalted butter
juice of 1 large orange

Crumble topping
150g plain flour
a pinch of salt
75g soft brown sugar
100g cold, unsalted butter, cut into chunks, plus extra for greasing

Preheat the oven to 180°C/gas 4. Put the quinces in a saucepan, cover with the water and add the caster sugar. Bring to simmering point, then cook until tender, adding more water if necessary to prevent the fruit from catching. Remove from the heat and drain off any excess water.

For the topping, sift the flour into a mixing bowl. Add the salt, brown sugar and butter. Massage with the tips of your fingers until the mixture resembles large crumbs; don't overwork it.

Place the quinces in an ovenproof dish greased with butter and add the pears, seeds from the vanilla pod, honey and lemon zest. Dot with the butter and pour over the orange juice. Spread the crumble mixture evenly on top. Bake for about 35 minutes or until the top is golden. Serve hot.

Goat's cheese with pecan nuts & honey

SERVES 1 (DOUBLE, TRIPLE, AND SO ON, ACCORDING TO HOW MANY YOU ARE SERVING)

PREP TIME: 5 MINUTES

There are three very different textures in this dessert. Firstly, you have the thick stickiness of the honey, which glides you in waves into the cold, creamy, fudgy smoothness of the cheese; then, when you bite into a pecan nut, it instantly sends its nutty shards spreading into the honey and cheese. I use Seggiano honey from Italy, which has a gorgeous topaz colour and is just the right consistency for this recipe.

150g goat's cheese
1 tablespoon orange flower honey
a handful of pecan nuts

If your goat's cheese is hard, crumble it over the honey and sprinkle with the pecan nuts. If using a soft, fresh goat's cheese, pour the honey over the cheese and sprinkle with the nuts.

Limoncello mascarpone

SERVES 4–6 / PREP TIME: 20 MINUTES PLUS 1 HOUR CHILLING

Limoncello is a lemon liqueur made on the Amalfi coast of Italy. It is absolutely delicious and combined with mascarpone makes a rich, creamy dessert. I recommend having small shot glasses of limoncello on the side to sip while you savour the limoncello mascarpone.

2 medium eggs, separated
2 tablespoons caster sugar
1 tablespoon grated lemon zest
250g mascarpone
1 tablespoon limoncello

In a mixing bowl, beat the egg whites until they will form peaks. In a separate bowl, beat the egg yolks, add the sugar and grated lemon zest and continue beating until light and creamy. Very gently whisk in the mascarpone and limoncello. Fold the egg whites through the mixture. Chill for 1 hour, then serve with biscotti and more limoncello.

Portuguese custard & saffron tarts

MAKES 6 / PREP TIME: 20 MINUTES / COOKING TIME: 10–14 MINUTES

Although I'd wanted to make these for a long time I always put the idea on the back burner. But eventually I drew a deep breath and had a go. It turns out they aren't a big deal to make and I was pleasantly surprised how close mine were to the real thing. I thought about giving a recipe for puff pastry, but it's so much easier buying it. I suggest you serve these with a large bowl of fruit on the table. Raspberries would fit the bill elegantly and you could even place a few on top of each little tart.

30g plain flour, plus extra for rolling out pastry
375g butter puff pastry, thawed if frozen
butter for greasing
650ml milk
4 medium egg yolks
a pinch of saffron threads
15g cornflour
110g caster sugar plus a little extra for sprinkling
4 tablespoons water

Preheat the oven to 230°C/gas 8. On a floured surface, roll out the puff pastry until you more or less have a 30cm square. Roll it up like Swiss roll, then cut it across into 2cm slices. Taking one slice at a time, lay it flat on the surface and press it out with a rolling pin or the palm of your hand. Ease the pastry into a muffin tray greased with butter, making sure the pastry extends a little beyond the rim. Repeat the process to make five more pastry cases.

For the custard, combine 150ml of the milk, the egg yolks, saffron, cornflour and plain flour in a bowl and whisk until smooth. Put the sugar and water in a saucepan and heat, stirring, until the sugar dissolves. Bring to the boil. Add the remaining milk and bring back to the boil. Making sure you stir constantly, slowly ladle the hot milk mixture into the flour mixture, then return everything to the pan. Cook on a moderate heat, stirring constantly, until the mixture thickens and becomes a thick custard.

Spoon the custard into the pastry cases to fill them by two-thirds, then sprinkle with a little extra caster sugar. Place immediately in the oven and bake for 10–14 minutes or until the custard is bubbling and has brown spots and the pastry is puffed. Remove from the oven and, when cool enough, transfer from the tins to a wire rack to cool completely.

Mexican flan with almond macaroons

SERVES 4–6 / PREP TIME: FLAN: 18 MINUTES PLUS AT LEAST 8 HOURS CHILLING; MACAROONS: 20 MINUTES PLUS 2 HOURS STANDING / COOKING TIME: FLAN: 30 MINUTES; MACAROONS: 15 MINUTES

This is a Mexican-inspired version of Crème Caramel. It's best to make it the day before so it has a good chance to set, but the morning of a dinner party should also work well. When serving, pour loads of cream on. If you want to make it a little more glamorous grate dark chocolate on the top with a little extra cinnamon. Serve with the almond macaroons below, or eat it with shortbread biscuits.

320g caster sugar
185ml water
1 cinnamon stick
6 medium eggs
1 teaspoon ground cinnamon, plus extra for decoration
200ml milk
284ml double cream
grated dark chocolate for decoration

Almond macaroons
160g blanched whole almonds
200g caster sugar
2 medium egg whites
butter for greasing
plain flour for dusting
icing sugar, sifted

Preheat the oven to 180°C/gas 4. Put 200g of the sugar, the water and the cinnamon stick in a saucepan and stir over a low heat until the sugar has dissolved. Bring to the boil and boil for about 8 minutes or until golden and the mixture has taken on a syrupy consistency. Remove the cinnamon, then pour the caramel into a deep ovenproof dish. Swirl to completely cover the bottom.

With an electric mixer, beat the eggs with the remaining sugar and ground cinnamon until frothy and pale. Combine the milk and cream in a saucepan and gently bring to boiling point. Pour into the egg mixture, beating constantly. Pour the mixture over the caramel and put into the oven. Bake for about 30 minutes or until the custard is set.

Remove from the oven and leave to cool, then cover and chill for at least 8 hours or overnight. To serve, run a knife around the edge of the custard and invert on to a serving plate. Decorate with grated chocolate and a dusting of cinnamon and serve with the macaroons.

For the macaroons, grind the almonds with 125g of the caster sugar in a food processor. In a mixing bowl, whisk the egg whites until stiff, then fold in the remaining caster sugar. Gently fold in the almond mixture, then spoon dollops on to a greased and floured baking sheet, spacing them well apart to allow for spreading. Flatten the mounds gently and dust with sifted icing sugar. Leave to stand for 2 hours, then bake for 15 minutes in a preheated 180°C/gas 4 oven.

Winter trifle with brandy custard, crystallised ginger, pistachio & caramelised pineapple

SERVES 4-6 / PREP TIME: 20 MINUTES / COOKING TIME: 15 MINUTES PLUS COOLING

This dish says Christmas to me: the rich velvetiness of custard and cream with an exotic touch of ginger, the fresh tartness of pineapple and the pale green and slight crunch of pistachios. The bowls will all certainly be left licked clean.

1 large pineapple, peeled and cut into cubes
2 teaspoons caster sugar
4 teaspoons brandy
500g home-made or good ready-made custard
4 heaped teaspoons stem ginger in syrup
500ml double cream, whipped
400g sponge finger biscuits
4 teaspoons chopped unsalted pistachios

Put the pineapple cubes in a frying pan and sprinkle over the sugar. Set on a high heat and cook until the sugar starts caramelising and the pineapple turns a golden brown. Leave it to cool.

Stir the brandy into the custard. Add the stem ginger and its syrup to the cream. Make a layer of sponge fingers on the bottom of a glass bowl. Spoon over an even layer of custard, followed by some caramelised pineapple and a sprinkling of pistachio nuts. Spoon over a layer of cream. Repeat the layers. Decorate the top with caramelised pineapple and a sprinkle of pistachios.

Profiteroles with hot chocolate sauce

SERVES 4–6 / PREP TIME: 30 MINUTES PLUS 2 HOURS CHILLING / COOKING TIME: 25 MINUTES

Profiteroles are small sweet or savoury buns made from choux paste. If they are sweet they are often filled with flavoured creams and covered in chocolate sauce. The name comes from the word 'profit', which originally meant a small gratuity or gift. I always make a few extra as it's hard for people to say no to more.

50g unsalted butter
150ml water
65g plain flour, sifted
a pinch of salt
2 large eggs, lightly beaten
284ml double cream
1 vanilla pod, split lengthways

Sauce
225g best-quality dark chocolate
142ml double cream

Preheat the oven to 220°C/gas 7. In a medium saucepan, combine the butter and the water. Heat gently until the butter melts, then bring to a rapid boil. Remove from the heat and add the sifted flour and salt. Beat thoroughly with a wooden spoon until the mixture is smooth and forms a ball. Transfer to a bowl and leave to cool for about 10 minutes, then slowly add the eggs to the mixture, beating well after each addition. It's important for the mixture to become a thick and shiny paste; if the eggs are added too quickly the cooked pastry will remain flat.

Spoon about 16 small mounds of the paste on to a large non-stick baking tray, spacing them well apart. Bake for about 20 minutes or until they have risen and are crisp and golden brown. Make a small hole in the side of each bun and return them to the oven for a further 5 minutes to dry out. Remove them to a wire rack to cool.

Whip the cream until thick, adding the seeds scraped from the vanilla pod. Pipe into each bun. Chill for 2 hours.

For the sauce, break the chocolate into a heatproof bowl set over a pan of hot water and melt gently. Remove from the heat and stir until smooth, then stir in the cream. Set aside. Before serving reheat the chocolate sauce, pour over the buns and serve.

Bitter chocolate mousse

SERVES 4-6 / PREP TIME: 30 MINUTES PLUS 1½ HOURS CHILLING

At first glance you may think this is a little old-fashioned, but it is a classic and classics never go out of style. Chocolate mousse is easy to make, it always looks like you've made an effort and it elicits those rewarding sighs from your guests on presentation. You can do all sorts of things to make it look even more appealing, such as serving it in a large bowl and decorating it with blueberries and mint, or in little individual pots with an espresso bean on top. Another idea is to decorate with chocolate shavings. I like to have a bowl of crème fraîche on the side; the bittersweet and sour make a wonderful combination. Otherwise serve with really good organic double cream or, even better, Jersey cream and let it fall in pleats into the chocolate folds. Mmmm...

250g best-quality dark bittersweet chocolate
50g unsalted butter, at room temperature
8 medium eggs, separated
a pinch of salt
cocoa powder, sifted
icing sugar, sifted (optional)

Break the chocolate into a saucepan and add the butter. Set over a very low heat and stir until melted and smoothly blended. Remove from the heat and place in the fridge to cool; don't let it get hard.

One at a time beat the egg yolks into the cooled chocolate mixture until thoroughly blended. In a mixing bowl, whisk the egg whites with a pinch of salt using an electric mixer until they form stiff peaks. Take a heaped spoonful of the egg whites and beat it energetically into the chocolate mixture, then fold the entire chocolate mixture into the rest of the stiff egg whites. Put into a serving bowl or individual dishes and chill for 1½ hours or until ready to serve. Dust the surface of the mousse with sifted cocoa powder and then with some sifted icing sugar, if you like.

Chocolate marquise with raspberries

SERVES 4–6 / PREP TIME: 20 MINUTES PLUS 3 HOURS CHILLING

Thank god chocolate is always in season so that we can rotate different fruits around it. If you fancy making this when raspberries are thin on the ground, opt for mandarins or tropical fruit such as papaya or mango instead. Use a really good chocolate such as Green and Black's.

100g best-quality dark chocolate
50g unsalted butter, softened
50g caster sugar
2 tablespoons cocoa powder
2 large egg yolks
1 teaspoon orange flower water
150ml double cream
fresh mint leaves for decoration
6 servings of raspberries, to serve

Line a 16cm round tin or an 8 x 22cm loaf tin with cling film. Break the chocolate into a heatproof bowl set over a pan of hot water and melt gently. Remove from the heat and stir until smooth.

In a mixing bowl, beat the butter with half the sugar until pale and fluffy. Sift in the cocoa and mix well. In another bowl, beat the egg yolks with the remaining sugar until pale and smooth, then add the orange flower water. In a third bowl, whip the cream until thick. Mix the melted chocolate into the butter mixture, then fold in the egg yolk mixture and, finally, fold in the cream. Spoon into the tin and chill for 3 hours or until set.

Turn out the marquise on to a serving dish and cut into four to six slices. Decorate with a couple of fresh mint leaves and serve with the raspberries or other fruit of choice.

Chocolate walnut brownies

SERVES 4–6 / PREP TIME: 15 MINUTES / COOKING TIME: 30–35 MINUTES PLUS COOLING

It's hard to resist a good chocolate brownie. Anything goes with them – they are sublime with thick double cream sprinkled with cinnamon or tart crème fraîche; with vanilla ice cream, even better with a chocolate sauce over it; or simply with a very smooth espresso to wash down the thick chocolate goo. Pecans are just as delightful as walnuts, or you can leave out the nuts altogether. With brownies, the more sticky and gungy in the middle, the better, so check them with a skewer inserted halfway between the middle and the edge (the skewer should come out clean here). I always eat them hot to warm. Why wait?

- 100g good-quality plain chocolate, finely chopped
- 125g unsalted butter, at room temperature, plus extra for greasing
- 275g caster sugar
- 1 teaspoon vanilla extract
- 2 large eggs, beaten
- 85g plain flour
- 2 tablespoons cocoa powder, preferably Green and Black's
- a pinch of fine sea salt
- 100g walnut halves

Preheat the oven to 180°C/gas 4. Break the chocolate into a heatproof bowl set over a saucepan of almost simmering water (do not let the water boil or the bottom of the bowl touch the water) and let it melt. Remove from the heat. Put the butter into a large mixing bowl and beat it until soft and creamy. Add the sugar and vanilla extract and continue beating until fluffy. Gradually beat in the eggs. Sift the flour, cocoa and salt on to the mixture, then spoon the melted chocolate on top and gently stir until it's all thoroughly mixed. Stir in the walnut halves.

Grease a 20cm square cake tin with butter and line the bottom with greaseproof paper. Pour in the brownie mixture and bake for 30–35 minutes. A dull crust should have formed on the top of the brownie. Remove from the tin when cool enough to handle and cut into large squares.

Peach & almond cake

SERVES 4–6 / PREP TIME: 30 MINUTES / COOKING TIME: 55 MINUTES

My daughter, Ithaka, came up with this recipe. It's a gooey, sticky, sweet, fruity and buttery dessert that melts in your mouth. There won't be a crumb left in sight.

175g unsalted butter, softened, plus extra for greasing
175g caster sugar
175g ground almonds
3 medium eggs, separated
1 teaspoon vanilla extract
2 large peaches, halved
double cream, to serve

Preheat the oven to 150°C/gas 2. With an electric mixer, cream the butter with the sugar. Add the ground almonds and beat until well integrated. Add the beaten egg yolks and vanilla extract, mixing in well. In a separate bowl, whisk the egg whites until stiff, then fold into the almond mixture.

Grease a 23 x 9.5cm baking tin with butter. Spoon in the mixture and put the peach halves on top. Bake for 30 minutes, then turn up the heat to 180°C/gas 4. Bake for another 25 minutes or until the top is golden. To check if it's ready, insert a skewer in the centre; it should come out clean. Serve warm with double cream.

Banana & date cake

SERVES 4–6 / PREP TIME: 15 MINUTES / COOKING TIME: 1½ HOURS

This cake is like a cousin to sticky toffee pudding. The dates become caramelised and toffee-like and the banana seems to melt and merge into the sponge. Nab it as soon as it's out of the oven, while it's still hot and steamy.

250g unsalted butter, melted, plus extra for greasing
5 medium eggs
250g soft brown sugar
250g self-raising flour, sifted
5 medium bananas, sliced
9 dates, pitted and finely chopped

Preheat the oven to 180°C/gas 4. Grease and line a 25cm loose-bottomed cake tin. With an electric mixer, lightly beat the eggs in a large bowl. Slowly add the sugar, flour and butter and beat until paler in colour. Fold in the bananas and dates, then pour into the prepared cake tin. Bake for 1½ hours or until a skewer stuck into the middle comes out clean. Serve immediately.

Panettone bread & butter pudding

SERVES 2 / PREP TIME: 30 MINUTES PLUS 20–30 MINUTES MARINATING

COOKING TIME: 45–50 MINUTES

Panettone is an Italian cake that is eaten throughout Italy on festive occasions. It often contains candied peel and raisins and sometimes nuts. It makes a wonderful bread and butter pudding. I've added a little citrus zest to this recipe, which gives the pudding a nice little zing and ping. It would also work well with a little tangerine zest instead of the orange and lemon.

1/2 large panettone
unsalted butter, at room temperature, plus extra for greasing
3 medium eggs
3 medium egg yolks
3 heaped tablespoons caster sugar
280ml double cream
400ml milk
grated zest of 1 orange
grated zest of 1 lemon
2 tablespoons Marsala
icing sugar, sifted

Cut the panettone thinly into slices like a cake. Butter each slice. Make a layer of slices, buttered side down, in a greased medium-sized, deep ovenproof dish. Then layer in the rest of the slices, buttered side up, until the dish is full. The slices will overlap.

Beat the eggs and egg yolks with the caster sugar in a mixing bowl, then beat in the cream, milk, citrus zest and Marsala. Pour over the buttered slices and leave for 20–30 minutes so the bread can absorb the liquid.

Preheat the oven to 180°C/gas 4. Sit the ovenproof dish in a large roasting tin in the middle of the oven and carefully pour enough boiling water into the tin to reach halfway up the sides of the pudding dish. Bake for 45–50 minutes or until the top is puffed and golden. Check after 35 minutes: if the top is becoming too brown cover loosely with aluminium foil. Depending on the size of your ovenproof dish it might take more or less time to cook. To check, lift up a piece of bread near the centre and insert a knife; if the pudding is set like custard it's ready. Leave to cool slightly until warm, then sprinkle with sifted icing sugar and serve with custard.

Index